Moulinex

FOOD PROCESSOR Cook Book

D1323986

INTRODUCTION

What is a Food Processor? 3
The Metal Blade 4
The Plastic Blade 8
Slicing, Grating & Chipping Discs 10
The Whisk 14
The Controls 16

RECIPES

Soups & Starters 17
Main Meals 25
Vegetables & Salads 41
Supper Snacks 49
Sauces & Dressings 57
Desserts 61
Bread, Cakes & Biscuits 77
Preserves 91

Recipe Index 94-95

The following symbols have been used in the recipes to indicate which food processor attachment should be used.

 METAL BLADE

 PLASTIC BLADE

 SLICING DISC

 CHIPPING DISC

 GRATING DISC

 WHISK

NOTES: THE RECIPES

★ Please follow either the metric or the imperial measures in the recipe section and be consistent, as they are not interchangeable.

★ All spoon measures are level, unless otherwise stated.

★ DO NOT OVERLOAD YOUR FOOD PROCESSOR. Check maximum quantities in your instruction leaflet and process in batches if necessary.

★ Unless otherwise stated, the recipes have been prepared with the food processor set on maximum speed.

What is a food processor?

Quite simply, it is a hard-working, versatile and compact work-top machine which takes all the hard work and much of the time out of food preparation.

With the minimum of attachments, your food processor will perform the functions of a mixer, blender, mincer, chopper, whisk and knife. And when you are more familiar with what it does, and how, you will wonder how you ever managed without it.

This book is designed to help you make the most of your Moulinex food processor. It contains illustrated step-by-step guides to the different processing techniques you can use, as well as a selection of carefully chosen recipes specially written for and tested on Moulinex machines.

When using your food processor for the first time, please read your instruction booklet thoroughly and get to know how it works. Then turn to page 4 of this book for a brief introduction to the food processor attachments and their uses.

Very quickly you will master your new kitchen appliance, getting to grips with its power and speed. You will become expert at judging processing time at a glance and in next to no time will be able to adapt your own favourite recipes.

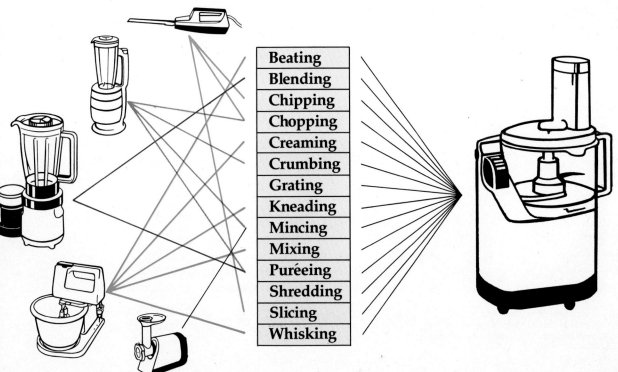

| Beating |
| Blending |
| Chipping |
| Chopping |
| Creaming |
| Crumbing |
| Grating |
| Kneading |
| Mincing |
| Mixing |
| Puréeing |
| Shredding |
| Slicing |
| Whisking |

METAL BLADE

The most versatile of your food processor attachments, the metal blade is used for chopping, mixing, mincing, blending, puréeing and making pastry and cake mixes. *NOTE:* it has razor sharp edges, so handle with care, and store in the bowl with the lid in place for safety.

CHOPPING

The metal blade can be used to chop all kinds of food to any consistency you choose, from a coarse texture for mince and terrines to the smoothest purée for soups, spreads and baby food.

To obtain the best results, food should first be cut into small even pieces (2-3cm/¾"-1¼") and then placed in the bowl. The chopping process is extremely fast, so to avoid over-processing operate the machine using the pulse button for only a few seconds at a time, and constantly check the results through the transparent lid.

As the metal blade is used to mix as well as chop ingredients, you have the advantage of being able to prepare many recipes in the same bowl; mincing meat, for example, then chopping herbs and breadcrumbs, and finally binding the mixture with an egg to make beefburgers.

NOTE: *It is not advisable to attempt to grind very hard food such as coffee beans or ice-cubes, as the blades may become blunt, and the bowl scratched.*

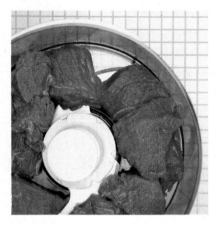

1. When chopping raw or cooked meat, cut off gristle, fat and skin, remove any bones and cut into even-size pieces before placing in the food processor bowl.

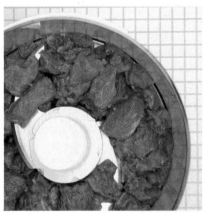

2. Process for a few seconds using pulse action to achieve a coarse texture for casseroles, curries, meatloaves and terrines.

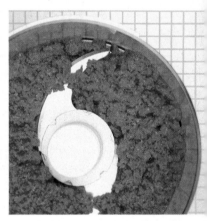

3. If you want a finer texture for pâtés and spreads, pulse for a few more seconds, but take care not to over-process, or you will end up with meat purée!

1. Liver takes even less time to chop, so process carefully using the pulse button (or a slow speed if you have a variable speed machine) ....

2. .... to achieve a coarse chop for rough pâtés.

3. .... and pulse for slightly longer to make purée for smooth liver pâté.

The metal blade makes light work of chopping fruit and vegetables for soups, stews and salads. Use it to process peeled and quartered onions, without tears.

2. Process for a few seconds to produce a coarse chop ....

3. .... and pulse a few more times for a finer consistency.

Fresh herbs such as parsley can be chopped coarsely or finely for garnishes, casseroles and herb butters. Also you can batch process and store in the fridge or freezer for later use.

You can use the metal blade to roughly chop soft fruit like tomatoes for casseroles and curries, or strawberries for fruit salad and jams.

Make your own fresh breadcrumbs for home made stuffings, and process stale cakes and biscuits into crumbs for flan bases and sweet crumbles. Oven-dry crumbs (raspings) and use on fried and grilled food, or for crispy toppings.

Take the hard work out of making home-made preserves by coarsely chopping citrus fruit for marmalades, and a variety of fruit, vegetables and berries for jams, pickles and chutneys.

All kinds of nuts can be processed with the metal blade; coarsely for salads and casseroles, finely for cakes and biscuits. And home-made peanut butter or exotic nut sauces couldn't be simpler to prepare.

Process tinned tuna fish and salmon for salads and kedgerees or finely for dips, spreads and rich pasta sauces.

BLENDING AND PUREEING

Using the metal blade, you can quickly purée all kinds of fruit, vegetables, meat and fish to make tasty soups, sauces, dips, drinks and desserts.

As with the chopping process, food to be blended or puréed should be even in size, and fairly small. It only takes a few seconds to purée soft and moist food like mushrooms and strawberries, slightly longer for hard food such as carrots and parsnips.

The food processor is so swift, you may find it worthwhile to process large quantities in batches, and freeze for future use.

NOTE: *When blending stock with cooked vegetables for soup, for example, or adding liquid to a purée for milk shakes or baby food, it is advisable to pulse the machine initially, to avoid excess splashing. If you have a variable speed food processor, start on the slowest speed setting and gradually increase speed as the liquid and solids are blended together.*

1. To make soup, strain off excess stock and place the cooked vegetables in the bowl. Process until coarsely chopped or puréed, according to the final consistency required.

2. With the machine running, gradually pour the reserved stock down the feed chute, making sure you do not exceed the maximum quantity advised for your machine.

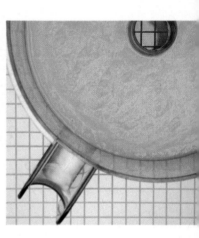

3. With little time and effort, you will have produced a delicious and nourishing soup which can be served immediately, or stored until required.

Purée apples to make fresh apple sauce for pork chops or puddings.

Fruits such as strawberries, gooseberries, stoned apricots and plums can be puréed to make sharp tangy sauces for exotic dressings, or for tasty fools, mousses and sorbets.

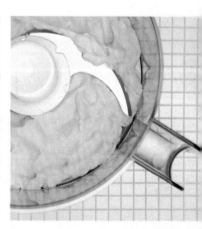

Create delicious dips and spreads by puréeing, for example, peeled and stoned avocado pears, then blending with cream, cottage cheese and mayonnaise.

MIXING PASTRY AND CAKES

Ising the metal blade, you can mix together
ngredients to make a vast array of dishes such as
ips, spreads, pâtés, sauces, stuffings and desserts.
est of all, you will be able to make
nouthwateringly light pastry almost at the touch of
 button for flans, pies, pasties and a host of dishes
rom simple week-day snacks to sophisticated
inner party fare.

ou can use either the metal or the plastic blade to
nake pastry, depending on the type of fat and its
emperature: the metal blade if the fat is cold and
ard and the plastic blade if the fat is soft or at room
emperature.

s a general rule, the colder the ingredients, the
etter the pastry, so when possible, use fat straight
rom the fridge and, if you have time, leave the bowl
nd blade in the fridge for 10 minutes beforehand.

1. Put flour, salt and cubed fat into the bowl, and pulse for
around 10 seconds, until the mixture resembles fine
breadcrumbs.

. With the processor running, gradually
ickle cold water down the feed chute to
ind the mixture, remembering that you
ill need less water than when you made
astry by hand.

3. Continue processing for a further 10
seconds, and stop as soon as the pastry
forms into dough. It is important not to
over-process, or the pastry will be dense
and tough. Remove from bowl, cover with
clingfilm, and chill for at least 30 minutes
before rolling out.

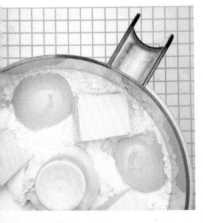

ollow this simple all-in-one
nethod to make cakes.

. Place all the ingredients in the bowl.

2. Process for around 15 seconds
(stopping if necessary to scrape down the
sides of the bowl with the specially
shaped spatula provided with the
machine) ....

3. ....until well mixed. Take care not to
over-process, or the cake will be heavy and
close-textured. Transfer the mixture to a
cake tin using the spatula.

7

PLASTIC BLADE

The white plastic blade, which is provided with some food processors, is used rather like a wooden spoon. Use it to take the lumps out of flour-based sauces, to make emulsified dressings, batters, buttercreams and icings. And use it to reduce dramatically the time and effort normally required to make bread and traditional cakes.

── MAKING BREAD ──

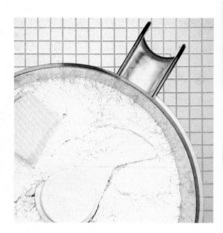

1. Mix the dry ingredients and fat lightly until they resemble fine breadcrumbs.

2. With the machine running, slowly pour the yeast liquid down the feed chute ....

3. ......and process until the mixture forms into a ball. Pulse for around 20 seconds to knead the dough, then remove, cover with clingfilm and leave in a warm place until risen. Repeat this process and leave to prove.

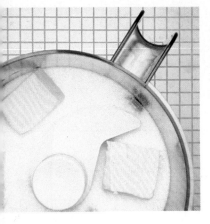

1. Place the sugar and fat in the bowl and......

2. .... process until light and fluffy.

3. Gradually add the beaten eggs through the feed chute.

4. Still on a slow speed setting, add the fruit and nuts down the feed chute and process......

5. ......gradually add the flour, and gently fold in on a slow speed setting......

6. ......until evenly folded into the cake mix.

DISCS

For slicing, grating and chipping vegetables and fruit, your food processor is an astonishing labour-saver, and dramatically reduces the time required particularly to prepare salads. It is possible, for example, to produce large quantities of coleslaw in seconds.

LOADING

The way that the food is stacked in the feed chute determines the quality and shape of the proccessed ingredients, so it is worth taking extra care when loading prior to processing.

If necessary, cut food to fit the feed chute, squaring off the ends to ensure they fit flush with the top of the disc.

Occasionally, you may find that pieces of food become trapped on top of the disc and are left unprocessed. This is normal, as a space is required between the disc and the lid. To minimise this, when processing larger quantities, refill the feed chute before it empties.

When slicing food, place upright in the feed chute, filling it completely, to ensure perfectly shaped slices.

If the feed chute is not packed correctly, the food may shift out of position during processing, resulting in elongated slices.

When grating, pack the food horizontally in the feed chute to produce long strips.

⊛ Food packed upright in the feed chute will result in a very short grate.

SLICING

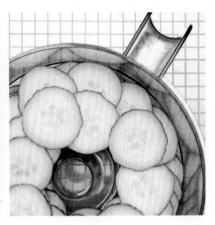

1. To slice vegetables like cucumber, carrots, courgettes and celery, prepare as advised, and pack upright in the feed chute.

2. Use the pusher — never your fingers — to press the food through the slicing disc, exerting even pressure (light for soft food like tomatoes, firm for hard food such as carrots)....

3. ....to ensure perfect results.

GRATING

1. To grate cheese, cut to fit the feed chute (or use leftovers straight from the fridge)........

2. ....press through the grating disc, using the pusher, refilling the feed chute before it is empty, if you are batch processing.

3. ....and use the cheese to make sauces, sandwiches and snacks, and to sprinkle onto soups for extra flavour.

CHIPPING

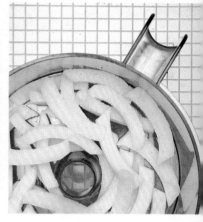

1. To chip potatoes or other root vegetables, prepare and pack horizontally in the feed chute ....

2. ....press through the chipping disc using the pusher........

3. ....to make gently curved chips ready for deep fat frying or adding to soup and stews.

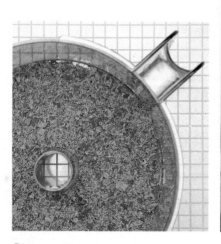

Grate or slice cabbage and add to grated carrots to produce coleslaw in seconds.

Grate chocolate for cooking and for decorating cakes and desserts.

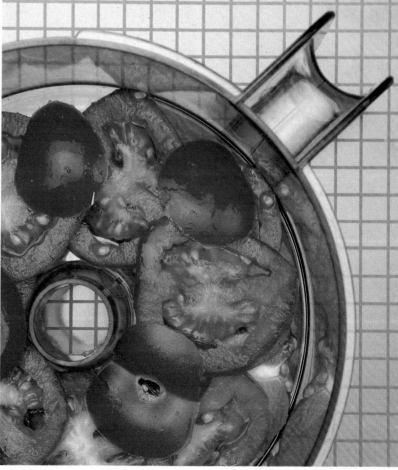

Soft fruit like tomatoes can be sliced with care.

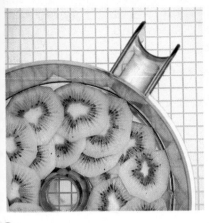

⊖ Use neatly sliced kiwifruit to add to salads and decorate dishes.

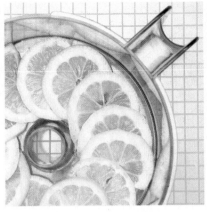

⊖ Slice citrus fruit for marinades and sauces, and freeze until required to garnish drinks.

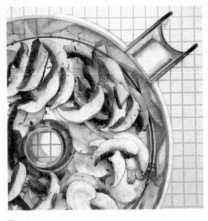

⊖ Slice button mushrooms to add to salads and stews.

⊖ Slice beetroot for salads and pickling.

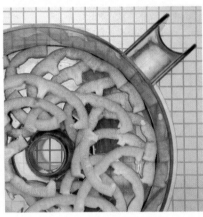

⊖ Slice peppers to add colour to salads and casseroles.

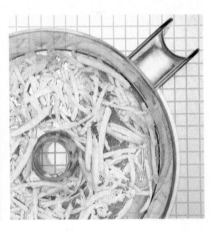

✳ Grate fresh ginger to add to cakes, biscuits and sauces.

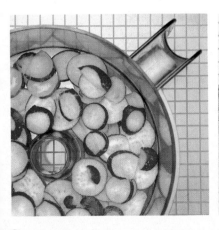

⊖ Slice radishes for use as a garnish or in salads.

✳ Use grated cheese for sauces and au gratin toppings.

⊖ Finely slice spring onions to use for garnishing dishes.

WHISK

The special whisk attachment can be used to blend ingredients for pouring sauces, batters, mayonnaise and dressings, and for whipping cream and egg whites.

To incorporate the maximum amount of air into mixes, always take the pusher out of the feed chute before switching on, and start on a slow speed, gradually increasing, if you have a variable speed food processor.

1. When whisking egg whites, make sure that the bowl and whisk attachment are clean, dry and free from grease before processing.

2. Whisk into a light and frothy consistency for folding into soufflés and mousses.

3. Slowly add sugar down the feed chute if you are making meringues ....

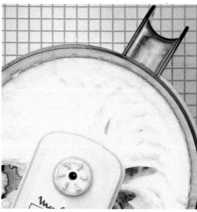

4. .... and whisk to stiff peaks.

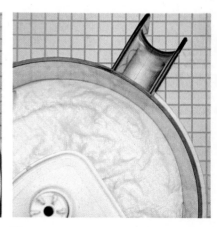

Use the whisk attachment to whip cream for featherlight mousses, or to pipe onto desserts and gateaux.

MAKING MAYONNAISE

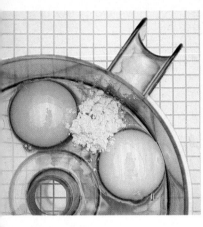

1. To make mayonnaise, place one egg and an additional egg yolk in the processor bowl, with 2.5ml/½ teaspoon dry mustard and seasoning, and process for 5 seconds.

2. With the machine running, slowly start dripping 275ml/½ pint olive oil down the feed chute, increasing the flow as the mixture thickens. Add 15ml/1 tablespoon wine vinegar and ....

3. .... with little time and effort, you will have whipped up thick, creamy and delicious home-made mayonnaise.

MAKING FATLESS SPONGES

With a variable speed food processor, you can also make fatless sponges using the whisk attachment, because on the slowest speed you can fold the flour gently into the whisked egg and sugar without knocking out all the air needed to create that light and fluffy texture.

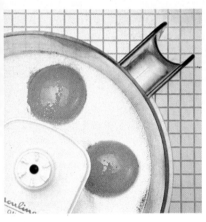

1. Place the caster sugar and eggs together in the processor bowl.

2. Whisk until the mixture is light and foaming, and at least doubled in volume. Set the processor on a slow speed and gradually add the flour·gently through the feed chute........

3. .... gently processing until all the flour is folded in. The sponge mix is now ready to transfer to a cake tin for baking.

15

The Controls

It is not only your choice of attachment which determines the processing results: an equally, if not more important factor is how you use the processor controls. Whether you use pulse or continuous action, for instance, can mean the difference between a coarse chop and smooth purée.

Before you try out any of the recipes in this book, you will find it worthwhile to re-read your instruction booklet. Practice using the pulse, continuous and (in some models) variable speed controls.

For Perfect Results – keep these points in mind:

Pulse Action

The pulse button operates the machine for as long as it is pressed down, allowing you to process foods in short bursts. This literally means pressing the button and letting go immediately, as if the button is too hot to touch!

Pulsing is used for high speed operations such as coarse chopping. It is particularly useful when you are new to the food processor and are learning how long it takes to process different foods: to avoid overprocessing you can pulse, then check the food and pulse again if necessary.

Continuous Action

For longer processing methods, like mixing or whisking, you can 'lock' your machine into the 'on' position so that it operates without you having to keep pressing down the pulse button, leaving you free to do something else.

Continuous action is useful when you want to add ingredients down the hopper while processing – making fruit cakes, or grating, slicing and chopping.

Variable Speed

The variable speed control is a feature on some of the Moulinex food processors. It operates rather like a dimmer switch and enables you to control the speed of the food processor, reducing or increasing it according to the task in hand.

You will find the variable speed control useful when blending ingredients for soups, batters or sauces: you can start on a slow speed and *gradually* build up speed to reduce splashing inside the bowl.

At the higher speeds you can incorporate more air into mixes. This is useful when preparing fatless sponges and also allows you to whisk egg whites to greater volume for meringues and soufflés.

At the lower speeds however, your food processor can carry out more gentle tasks like folding in flour when preparing a traditional cake mix (at higher speeds you would beat out the air, giving a close texture and heavy cake).

This increased control that you have when using your food processor leads to optimum results. Practice the use of your variable speed control so that you get the most from this facility.

Cream of Watercress Soup

1 medium onion, peeled and quartered
2 bunches of watercress
50g 2oz butter
40g 1½oz plain flour
850ml 1½ pints chicken stock
250ml ½ pint milk
salt and pepper
150ml ¼ pint double cream

 Place the onion in the processor bowl and chop finely.

Add the watercress and chop finely.

Melt the butter, add the onion and watercress and fry for 5 minutes until soft.

Add the flour and stir until absorbed. Remove from heat.

Gradually stir in the chicken stock and milk, then return to the heat and stir until the soup thickens. Season to taste and simmer for 20 minutes.

Serve with a swirl of cream on top and watercress sprigs.

Minestrone Soup

1 medium leek, washed
1 medium onion, peeled and quartered
2 sticks celery, washed
30ml 2tbsp oil
30ml 2tbsp plain flour
1 litre 2 pints chicken stock
2 carrots, peeled
4 tomatoes, peeled
200g 8oz ham, diced
25g 1oz small pasta shapes
salt and pepper

Slice the leeks, onion and celery in the processor.

Heat the oil and fry the sliced vegetables until soft.

Stir in the flour.

Gradually add the chicken stock and stir until thickened.

 Coarsely grate the carrots.

 Chop the tomatoes.

Add both the carrots and tomatoes to the soup with the ham and pasta shapes, and season to taste.

Bring to the boil, stirring occasionally, and simmer for 20 minutes until the vegetables are cooked.

Serve with French bread and Parmesan cheese.

Mushroom Soup

1 small onion, peeled and quartered
225g 8oz **button mushrooms**
25g 1oz **butter**
25g 1oz **plain flour**
575ml 1pint **chicken stock**
275ml ½ pint **milk**
salt and pepper
150ml ¼ pint **single cream**
parsley to garnish

 Place the onion in the processor bowl and chop finely.

 Wipe the mushrooms and slice into the bowl.

Melt the butter in a saucepan and cook the onions and mushrooms over a low heat for 5 minutes, stirring well.

Stir in the flour and cook for 2 minutes adding the stock and milk, stir well and bring to the boil.

Season well, cover and simmer for 20 minutes.

 Return soup to the processor bowl and blend.

Stir in the cream and heat gently. Do not boil. Garnish with a mushroom slice and parsley.

Gazpacho

50g 2oz **crustless white bread**
30ml 2tbsp **wine vinegar**
1 **garlic clove**, peeled
1 large **onion**, peeled and cut into 8 pieces
1 green **pepper**, de-seeded and cut into 6 pieces
1 **cucumber**, peeled and cut into 2cm 1" slices
60ml 4tbsp **olive oil**
1kg 2lb **tomatoes**, peeled and de-seeded
150ml ¼ pint **tomato juice**
salt and pepper

 Break the bread into pieces and place in the processor bowl and chop finely.

Add the vinegar, garlic, onion, half the pepper and half the cucumber and process until smooth.

Gradually add the oil down through the feeder tube (using low speed setting if you have a variable speed model).

Add the tomatoes and tomato juice, season to taste and process until smooth. Chill.

 Chop the remaining cucumber and pepper and serve with the soup.

Garnish with small fried croutons and ice cubes.

Chicken Soup

1 medium onion, peeled and quartered
2 carrots
1 stick celery, washed and trimmed
25g 1oz **butter**
25g 1oz **plain flour**
850ml 1½ pints **chicken stock**
150ml ¼ pint **milk**
salt and pepper
100g 4oz **cooked chicken**
30ml 2tbsp **double cream**
chives to garnish

Slice the onion, carrots and celery into the processor bowl.

Melt the butter in a saucepan and cook the vegetables over a low heat for 5 minutes, stirring well.

Stir in the flour and cook for 2 minutes, adding the stock and milk, stir well and bring to the boil.

Season well, cover and simmer for 20 minutes.

Return the soup to the processor bowl and blend until smooth.

Add the chicken and cream and process for 10 seconds.

Return soup to the saucepan and heat gently, do not boil. Garnish with chopped chives.

Tomato Soup

1 small onion, peeled and quartered
25g 1oz **butter**
450g 1lb **tomatoes**
25g 1oz **plain flour**
575ml 1 pint **beef stock**
salt and pepper
30ml 2tbsp **tomato pureé**
15ml 1tbsp **Worcestershire sauce**
pinch paprika
2.5ml ½tsp **sugar**
150ml ¼ pint **double cream**

Place the onion in the processor bowl and chop finely.

Melt the butter in a saucepan and cook the onions over a low heat for 5 minutes, stirring well.

Skin the tomatoes by dipping them in boiling water. Cut them into quarters and discard the pips.

Roughly chop the tomato flesh and add to the onions.

Stir in the flour and cook for 2 minutes, adding the stock, seasoning, tomato puree, Worcestershire sauce, paprika and sugar.

Bring to the boil, then cover and simmer for 30 minutes.

Return the soup to processor bowl and blend until smooth.

Reheat soup gently and just before serving swirl the cream into the centre. Decorate with parsley.

Turkey Pâté

3 bay leaves
6 rashers streaky bacon, derinded
50g 2oz crustless white bread
350g 12oz raw turkey meat, diced
200g 8oz lean pork, diced
1 small onion, peeled and quartered
2 garlic cloves
2.5ml ½tsp dried thyme
30ml 2tbsp sherry
salt and pepper

Put the bay leaves in the bottom of a 450g (1lb) loaf tin.

Stretch the bacon using the back of a knife and use to line the tin.

 Place the bread in the processor bowl and chop finely.

Add all the other ingredients and process until combined.

Turn into the tin and level the top. Cover with foil.

Stand in a pan half filled with water and bake at 180°C, 350°F, Gas No. 4 for 1½ hours.

Cool in the tin, then place weights on the surface and leave until firm.

Turn out and slice to serve.

Veal & Orange Terrine

1 small onion, peeled and quartered
1 garlic clove, peeled
700g 1½lb stewing veal, diced
200g 8oz lean pork, diced
2 oranges
salt and pepper
15g ½oz powdered gelatine
45ml 3tbsp cold water
250ml ½ pint beef stock, strained

 Place the onion, garlic, veal, pork, grated rind of 1 orange and seasoning in the processor bowl, and process until finely chopped.

Press into a 1·2 litre (2 pint) terrine dish, cover with foil and stand in a pan half-filled with water.

Cook at 180°C, 350°F, Gas No. 4 for 1½ hours.

When cooked pour off the liquid, and replace foil. Place weights on the top until firm.

Slice the other orange and arrange on the terrine.

Dissolve the gelatine in water, add to the stock and pour into the dish covering the orange. Chill to set.

Chicken Liver Pâté

Smoked Mackerel Spread

Chicken Liver Pâté

1 onion, peeled and quartered
1 garlic clove, peeled
100g 4oz butter
500g 1lb chicken livers
60ml 4tbsp double cream
30ml 2tbsp thick mayonnaise
salt and pepper
25g 1oz butter, melted

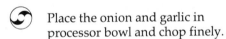 Place the onion and garlic in processor bowl and chop finely.

Heat the butter in a saucepan and add the onion, garlic and chicken livers and fry until just cooked about 15 minutes. Allow to cool.

Return to the processor bowl, add the cream, mayonnaise and seasoning and process until smooth.

Pour into a serving dish and smooth over the top. Chill until set.

Pour melted butter over the top and chill.

Serve with toast.

Smoked Mackerel Spread

100g 4oz cream cheese
45ml 3tbsp lemon juice
200g 8oz smoked mackerel fillets, skinned
salt and pepper
parsley and lemon twists to garnish

Place all the ingredients in the processor bowl and process until they are combined.

Spoon into a serving dish and chill.

Garnish with parsley and lemon twists.

Serve with savoury biscuits.

If you want to ring the changes, try **Smoked Haddock** instead.

 Place 350g (12oz) smoked haddock, cooked and skinned, with 100g (4oz) cream cheese, 15ml (1tbsp) lemon juice and process until smooth. Check for seasoning, then chill, garnish with parsley sprigs and serve with toast or savoury biscuits.

Mixed Cheese Spread

5 parsley sprigs
100g 4oz **mature Cheddar cheese, cubed**
100g 4oz **Red Leicester cheese, cubed**
100g 4oz **cream cheese**
15ml 1tbsp **French mustard**
50g 2oz **softened butter**
parsley to garnish

 Place parsley sprigs in processor bowl and chop finely.

Add the Cheddar and Red Leicester cheeses and chop finely.

Add the cream cheese, mustard and butter and process until evenly mixed.

Spoon the mixture into a serving dish, smooth the top and chill.

Garnish with parsley.

Serve with crackers or toast.

Anchovy Pepper Dip

75g 3oz **crustless white bread**
½ **green pepper, de-seeded, cut into 4**
50g 2oz **can anchovy fillets, drained**
142ml 5fl oz **carton soured cream**
45ml 3tbsp **thick mayonnaise**
15ml 1tbsp **lemon juice**
15ml 1tbsp **Worcestershire sauce**
salt and pepper

 Break the bread into pieces and place in the processor bowl and chop finely.

Add the green pepper and anchovy fillets, and process again until well blended.

Add the soured cream, mayonnaise, lemon juice and Worcestershire sauce and process until combined. Season to taste.

Serve with thin sticks of carrot and celery, cauliflower florets and button mushrooms.

Salami Dip

150g 6oz **cream cheese**
30ml 2tbsp **wine vinegar**
30ml 2tbsp **olive oil**
15ml 1tbsp **Worcestershire sauce**
5ml 1tsp **dry mustard**
salt and pepper
75g 3oz **salami, de-rinded**
30ml 2tbsp **mayonnaise**
15ml 1tbsp **tomato ketchup**

 Place all the ingredients in processor bowl, and process until smooth.

Check for seasoning, then chill.

Serve with small savoury biscuits.

Stilton & Celery Spread

2 sticks **celery, cut into pieces**
4 **spring onions, halved**
50g 2oz **Stilton cheese**
100g 4oz **cream cheese**
50g 2oz **butter**
6 slices **dark rye bread**
12 **orange segments**
9 **black grapes, halved**

 Place the celery and onions in the bowl and chop finely.

Add the Stilton, cream cheese and butter, and process to combine all ingredients.

Spread the mixture evenly over the slices of bread.

Garnish each with the two orange segments and three grape halves.

Main Meals

Harvest Hotpot

75g 3oz **crustless white bread**
500g 1lb **stewing steak, diced**
2.5ml ½tsp **oregano**
salt and pepper
30ml 2tbsp **oil**
447g 15¾oz **can of baked beans**
150ml ¼ pint **beef stock**
30ml 2tbsp **tomato ketchup**
300g 12oz **potatoes, peeled**
25g 1oz **butter**

 Break the bread into the processor bowl and chop finely. Add the meat, oregano and seasoning, and process until smooth.

Form the mixture into balls, 2·5cm (1") in diameter.

Heat the oil and fry the meatballs until evenly browned and place in a 1·2 litre (2 pint) pie dish and stir in the beans, stock and ketchup.

 Slice the potatoes and arrange around the edge of the dish. Dot with butter and season.

Bake at 200°C, 400°F, Gas No. 6 for 45 minutes.

Spicy Lamb Bake

1 large **onion peeled and quartered**
1 **garlic clove**
500 g 1lb **cooked lamb, cubed**
30ml 2tbsp **oil**
63g 2¼oz **can tomato purée**
150ml ¼ pint **stock**
30ml 2tbsp **paprika**
15ml 1tbsp **Worcestershire sauce**
salt and pepper
500g 1lb **courgettes**
200g 8oz **Edam cheese, grated**

 Place the onion and garlic in the processor bowl and chop finely.

Add the cooked lamb and chop finely.

Heat the oil in the pan, add the onion and lamb mixture and fry for 5 minutes.

Add the tomato pureé, stock, paprika, Worcestershire Sauce and seasoning and stir well

 Slice the courgettes

Grate the Edam cheese.

Place half the meat mixture in a 1·4 litre (2½ pint) shallow ovenproof dish. Cover with half the courgettes and half the cheese. Repeat layers.

Place in an oven 190°C, 375°F, Gas No. 5 for about 30 minutes.

Kofta Kebabs

1 small onion peeled and quartered
500g 1lb boneless shoulder lamb, diced
1 size 3 egg
5ml 1tsp ground allspice
salt and pepper
25g 1oz flour
1 red pepper, de-seeded, cut into 12 pieces
1 green pepper, de-seeded, cut into 12 pieces

 Place the onion in the processor bowl and chop finely.

Add the lamb, egg, spice and seasoning and process until smooth.

Flour your hands and mould the mixture into 18 short sausage shapes. Thread three 'sausages' onto each of six flat-bladed skewers, alternating with the pepper pieces.

Grill under a moderate heat, turning frequently, for 10 minutes until the Kofta Kebabs are evenly browned and cooked through.

Serve each skewer on a bed of rice.

Porkies in Onion Sauce

500g 1lb lean pork, diced
100g 4oz streaky bacon, diced
1.25ml ¼tsp mixed herbs
salt and pepper
oil for frying
2 medium onions peeled and quartered
25g 1oz butter
500ml 1 pint white sauce

 Place the pork, bacon, herbs and seasoning in the processor bowl and process until the ingredients are finely chopped. Divide and shape into 16 balls.

Heat the oil in a pan and gently fry the meatballs until evenly browned. Keep warm.

 Slice the onions.

Heat the butter, add the onions and fry until soft. Add to the white sauce and reheat.

Serve the meatballs on a bed of ribbon noodles and pour the onion sauce over.

Steak & Kidney Pie

450g 1lb **stewing steak, fat removed, cubed**
175g 6oz **kidney**
275ml ½pt **beef stock**
1 large **onion peeled and quartered**
30ml 2tbsp **plain flour**
2 **oxo cubes, crumbled**
350g 12oz **plain flour**
pinch salt
175g 6oz **hard margarine**
water to mix

 Place the stewing steak and kidney in the processor bowl and roughly chop.

Toss in the flour and place into a large saucepan.

Place the onion in the food processor and finely chop. Add to the steak and kidney in the saucepan.

Add the beef stock and crumbled oxo cubes and seasoning to the steak and kidney and bring to the boil. Lower the heat and simmer gently for 1¾-2 hours (or until meat is tender). Allow to cool.

 Place the flour, salt and margarine in the processor bowl and follow method on page 7.

Divide pastry in half and roll out one half to cover a 20cm (8") pie plate.

Pile the cooked steak and kidney into the centre and moisten the edges of the pastry with water.

Roll out remaining pastry and cover the pie, pressing the edges well together to seal.

Brush top of pie with milk and bake in the centre of the oven at 220°C, 425°F, Gas No. 7 for 20 to 30 minutes or until golden brown.

Boeuf en Croûte

250g 9oz **plain flour**	25g 1oz **butter, softened**
pinch **salt**	50g 2oz **smooth liver pâté**
225g 8oz **butter**	5ml 1tsp **ground thyme**
water to mix	1 size 3 **egg**
1.4kg 3lb **fillet of beef**	15ml 1tbsp **oil**
garlic clove	

Sift flour and salt into processor bowl.

Add half of the butter and process together for 10 seconds, until the mixture resembles fine breadcrumbs.

Add sufficient water to mix to a soft dough ball. Chill.

Place remaining butter between 2 sheets of greaseproof paper. Roll out a rectangle about 13cm x 8cm/5" x 3".

On a lightly floured surface, roll out dough to a rectangle shape about 25cm x 20cm/10" x 8". Place rolled butter in the middle of the dough. Fold in the top and bottom thirds of the dough to enclose butter in parcel.

Give the dough a half turn so that the side seam is on your left, sealing edges well. Roll into a rectangle again and fold in top and bottom thirds of dough as before. Wrap and chill pastry for 15 minutes.

Repeat rolling, turning and folding pastry 4 more times, chilling between rollings.

Trim any fat from fillet, roll it into a neat shape.

Cut the garlic clove into slivers and insert them into the beef with the point of a sharp knife.

Spread the softened butter over the top of the fillet and cook meat for 10 minutes in a roasting tin in the oven set at 220°C/425°F/Gas no.7. Remove beef from oven and leave to cool.

Roll out the prepared puff pastry to an oblong 3½ times the width of the fillet and 18cm/7" longer than the length.

Spread the pâté over the top of the fillet, place the meat, pâté side down in the centre of the pastry and sprinkle with thyme.

Fold the pastry over and under the meat, brushing the seams with water and sealing edges thoroughly.

Turn the pastry over so that the join is underneath. Prick the top with a fork and decorate with leaves cut from pastry trimmings. Chill.

Beat the egg with the oil and brush it over the pastry to glaze during cooking.

Stand the pastry roll on a wet baking tray and bake in the oven for 35 minutes on 220°C/425°F/Gas No.7. The pastry should then be golden brown.

Apricot & Walnut Lamb

1½kg 3lb **boned shoulder of lamb**
salt and pepper
150g 6oz **crustless white bread**
1 small **onion peeled and quartered**
100g 4oz **dried apricots**
75g 3oz **walnuts**
1 size 3 **egg**

Season the inside of the shoulder of lamb joint.

 Break the bread into pieces and place in the processor bowl and chop finely.

Add the onion, apricots, walnuts and seasoning and process until finely chopped.

Add the egg and process to mix.

Stuff the lamb joint, secure with string and roast at 190°C, 375°F, Gas No. 5 for 2 hours, basting occasionally during cooking.

Capon with Bacon & Celery Stuffing

150g 6oz **crustless, white bread**
8 **parsley sprigs**
1 **medium onion, peeled and quartered**
200g 8oz **streaky bacon, diced**
2 **sticks celery, cut into pieces**
45ml 3tbsp **lemon juice**
1 **size 3 egg, beaten**
salt and pepper
2½kg 5lb **oven-ready capon**
25g 1oz **butter, melted**

 Break the bread into pieces and place in the processor bowl, add the parsley and chop finely.

Add the onion, bacon and celery and chop finely.

Add the lemon juice, egg and seasoning and process to mix.

Stuff the neck cavity of the capon with half the stuffing and secure with string.

Roll the remaining stuffing into 8 balls.

Brush the capon with melted butter, season and roast at 180°C, 350°F, Gas No. 4 allowing 25 minutes per 500g (1lb) plus 25 minutes.

Add the stuffing balls for the last 30 minutes.

Lamb Curry

1 onion peeled and quartered
700g 1½lbs **boned lamb, cut into pieces**
30ml 2tbsp **oil**
5ml 1tsp **curry powder**
salt and pepper
clove garlic, peeled, crushed
2.5ml ½tsp **cinnamon**
pinch cumin
pinch powdered ginger
pinch corriander
225ml 8fl oz **stock**
bouquet garni
1 green pepper, de-seeded
100g 4oz **button mushrooms**
1 small banana, peeled
150ml 5fl oz **natural yoghurt**

Place the onion in the processor bowl and chop finely, remove.

Put the lamb pieces into the processor bowl and roughly chop.

Heat the oil in a pan and fry the onions and meat.

Add the curry powder, seasoning and spices and cook for 2 minutes.

Stir in the stock and bouquet garni, and cook for 40 minutes.

Slice the green pepper, mushrooms and banana, add all the ingredients to the curry mixture and cook for a further 10 minutes.

Remove bouquet garni and serve with boiled rice.

Country Style Pork

2kg 4lb **belly of pork, boned**
75g 3oz **crustless white bread**
6 large parsley sprigs
50g 2oz **pitted prunes**
1 small onion peeled and halved
1 dessert apple, peeled and cored
15ml 1tbsp **lemon juice**
salt and pepper

Make a cavity for stuffing in the meat from where the bones were removed.

 Break the bread into pieces and place in the processor bowl. Add the parsley and prunes, chop finely and put to one side.

 Grate the onion and apple coarsely and mix into the crumb mixture with the lemon juice and seasoning.

Stuff the joint and secure with string. Sprinkle the skin with salt and roast the joint skin side up, at 220°C, 425°F Gas No. 4 for 20 minutes, then at 180°C, 350°F, Gas No. 4 for about 2 hours or until tender.

Veal & Bacon Loaf

150g 6oz **crustless white bread**
1 medium **onion peeled and quartered**
700g 1½lb **stewing veal, diced**
200g 8oz **streaky bacon, diced**
2.5ml ½tsp **mixed herbs**
salt and pepper
tomato sauce

 Break the bread into pieces, place in the processor bowl and chop finely.

Add the onion, veal, bacon, mixed herbs and seasoning and process until coarsely chopped.

Spoon the mixture into a 900g 2lb loaf tin and cover with foil.

Bake at 180°C, 350°F, Gas No. 4 for 1 hour.

Serve sliced with home-made tomato sauce.

Chicken Risotto

2 **parsley sprigs**
1 medium **onion peeled and quartered**
1 **red pepper, de-seeded, cut into 6 pieces**
30ml 2tbsp **oil**
100g 4oz **button mushrooms**
100g 4oz **peas**
350g 12oz **cooked chicken, diced**
350g 12oz **cooked long-grain rice**
15ml 1tbsp **chilli sauce**
salt and ground black pepper
lemon twists and parsley to garnish

 Place the parsley in the processor bowl, and chop finely. Reserve.

Place the onion and red pepper in the processor bowl and chop finely.

Heat the oil in a pan and fry the chopped onion and pepper until soft.

 Slice the mushrooms, add to the onions and fry for a further 2 minutes.

Add the chopped parsley, peas, diced chicken, cooked rice and chilli sauce, and season to taste. Fry gently to reheat, 15 minutes.

Garnish with lemon twists and parsley sprigs.

Crusty Pork Chops

4 pork loin chops
salt and pepper
75g 3oz **crustless white bread**
4 parsley sprigs
1 medium onion peeled and quartered
30ml 2tbsp **tomato ketchup**

Season the chops and cook under a moderate grill for 10 minutes on one side.

 Break the bread into pieces and place in the processor bowl.

Add the parsley and the onion and chop finely.

Add the tomato ketchup and seasoning and process until the ingredients are combined.

Turn the chops over and cook for 5 minutes.

Divide the topping between the chops and cook for a further 5 minutes or until the topping is golden brown.

Cannelloni

50g 2oz **crustless white bread**
2 large parsley sprigs
200g 8oz **cooked, lean beef, diced**
100g 4oz **streaky bacon, diced**
1 small onion peeled and quartered
30ml 2tbsp **tomato purée**
salt and pepper
12 cannelloni rolls
400ml ¾ pint **white sauce**
75g 3oz **Cheddar cheese**

 Break the bread into pieces and place in the processor bowl. Add the parsley and chop finely.

Add the diced beef, bacon, onion, tomato purée and seasoning, and process until all the ingredients are combined.

Use the mixture to fill the uncooked cannelloni rolls.

Place in a 1·2 litre (2 pint) shallow ovenproof dish and pour over the sauce.

 Grate the Cheddar cheese and sprinkle over the cannelloni.

Bake at 190°C, 375°F, Gas No. 5 for 30-35 minutes.

Smokey Fish Crumble

1 medium onion, peeled and quartered
50g 2oz **butter**
50g 2oz **plain flour**
500ml 1 pint **milk**
10ml 2tsp **lemon juice**
3 size 3 eggs, **hard-boiled, halved**
700g 1½lb **smoked haddock, cooked and skinned**
salt and pepper
100g 4oz **plain flour**
50g 2oz **butter**
50g 2oz **Cheddar cheese**

 Place the onion in the processor bowl and chop finely.

Heat the butter and fry the onion until soft.

Stir in the flour and gradually add the milk, stirring until the sauce thickens.

Pour the onion sauce into the processor bowl, add the lemon juice, eggs and fish and process until combined. Season. Turn into a 1·7 litre (3 pint) ovenproof dish.

Place the flour and a pinch of salt in the processor bowl, add the fat and cheese, chop finely. Sprinkle over the fish mixture.

Bake at 190°C, 375°F, Gas No. 5 for 35 minutes until golden brown.

Plaice Curry

1 medium onion peeled and quartered
30ml 2tbsp oil
10ml 2tsp curry powder
2 tomatoes, skinned
2 apples, peeled and cored
30ml 2tbsp raisins
275ml ½pt single cream
salt and pepper
4 plaice fillets skinned and rolled

Place the onion in the processor bowl and chop finely.

Heat the oil in a frying pan and fry the onion until transparent.

Add the curry powder and cook for a further minute.

Place the tomatoes and apples into the processor bowl and roughly chop.

Add the tomatoes, apple, raisins, cream and salt and pepper to the prepared onions, stirring well. Cover dish and cook for 8 minutes, stirring occasionally.

Add the plaice fillets to the mixture and cook for a further 8 minutes.

Serve with saffron rice.

Fish & Chips

4 large potatoes, peeled
100g 4oz plain flour
pinch of salt
1 size 3 egg
275ml ½pt milk
4 cod fillets
flour to coat

 Place the potatoes into the feed chute and process. Put into a bowl of cold water to remove the starch and to prevent the chips from turning brown.

 Put the flour and salt into the processor bowl and mix for 5 seconds.

Add the remaining liquid and mix for a further few seconds. Pour into a large bowl.

Coat the cod fillets in flour and shake off any excess.

Heat the oil in a deep fat fryer to 190°C. Dip fish in prepared batter and fry turning during cooking until a light golden brown. Drain on absorbent kitchen paper.

Dry chips thoroughly and fry until a light golden brown. Drain on absorbent kitchen paper.

Serve with a wedge of lemon and tartare sauce.

Plaice Rollups
with Cucumber Sauce

8 plaice fillets, skinned
salt and pepper
100g 4oz **crustless white bread**
6 parsley sprigs
100g 4oz **peeled prawns**
15ml 1tbsp **lemon juice**
1 small onion peeled and quartered
10cm 4" **length of cucumber**
25g 1oz **butter**
15g ½oz **flour**
150ml ¼ pint **single cream**

Season the plaice fillets.

 Break the bread into pieces and place in the processor bowl. Add the parsley, prawns and lemon juice and chop coarsely.

Divide the mixture between the plaice fillets and roll up, beginning with the tail end.

Place in an ovenproof dish, dot with butter and cover.

Bake at 180°C, 350°F, Gas No. 4 for 15-20 minutes.

 For the sauce, chop the onion and cucumber in the processor and fry in butter for 8 minutes.

Add the flour and cook for 1 minute then add the cream. Heat gently. Season.

Serve the sauce with the plaice.

Fish & Mushroom Bake

200g 8oz **button mushrooms**
50g 2oz **butter**
2 tomatoes, quartered
4 frozen fish steaks
298g 10½oz **can condensed mushroom soup**
120ml 8tbsp **milk**
100g 4oz **self-raising flour**
pinch salt
25g 1oz **margarine, cubed**
45-60ml 3-4 tbsp **milk**

Slice the mushrooms using the slicing disc.

Heat the butter in a pan and fry the mushrooms until soft. Place in a 1·2 litre (2 pint) ovenproof dish.

Place the tomatoes in the processor bowl fitted with metal blade and chop finely. Spoon on top of the mushrooms. Add the fish.

Warm the condensed mushroom soup with the milk and pour over the fish steaks.

Place the flour and salt in the processor bowl. Add the margarine and chop finely.

Add the milk gradually down the feed chute while pulsing the processor, until the mixture forms into a soft dough.

Roll out to 1·2cm (½ inch) thick, cut into 8 x 3cm (1½ inch) rounds and place on the fish.

Bake at 190°C, 375°F, Gas No. 5 for 30 minutes.

Vegetables & Salads

Cheesy Scalloped Potatoes

1kg 2lb **potatoes, peeled**
1 medium **onion, peeled and quartered**
100g 4oz **Cheddar cheese**
25g 1oz **butter**
salt and pepper
1 size 3 egg
250ml ½ pint **milk**

 Slice the potatoes.

 Grate the onion and cheese.

Arrange the potato slices in a well-buttered, shallow ovenproof dish and sprinkle each layer with onion, cheese and salt and pepper. Finish with a thick layer of cheese and dot with butter.

Beat the egg and milk together and pour carefully over the potatoes.

Cover the dish with foil and bake at 180°C, 350°F, Gas No. 4 for 1½ hours or until the potatoes are cooked and the topping is golden.

Savoury Potato Patties

700g 1½lb **potatoes, peeled**
1 small **onion, peeled and quartered**
100g 4oz **streaky bacon, derinded and diced**
30ml 2tbsp **plain flour**
1 size 3 egg
salt and pepper
oil for frying

 Grate the potatoes and onions and set aside.

 Place the bacon in the processor bowl and chop finely.

Mix the potatoes, onions, bacon, flour and egg until combined and season to taste.

Shape into 6 x 7.5cm (3 inch) rounds.

Heat the oil in a pan. Fry the rounds for about 15 minutes, turning once until golden. Drain.

Serve on their own or with scrambled egg.

Stir-fried Vegetables

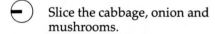

150g 6 oz **white cabbage**
1 large **onion**, peeled and quartered
100g 4oz **button mushrooms**
300g 12oz **cooked chicken**, diced
2 large **carrots**
45ml 3tbsp **oil**
30ml 2tbsp **soy sauce**
lemon and tomato wedges to garnish

 Slice the cabbage, onion and mushrooms.

Place to one side in a large bowl, add the diced cooked chicken, and mix well.

Grate the carrots using the processor.

Heat the oil in a large frying pan, add the chicken and vegetable mixture, and fry for 5 minutes, stirring continuously.

Add the grated carrot and soy sauce and stir fry for a further 5 minutes.

Transfer to a serving dish and garnish with lemon and tomato wedges. Serve immediately.

Leeks in Mustard Sauce

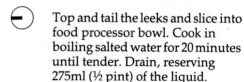

900g 2lb **leeks**, washed
225g 8oz **cheese**
275ml ½ pint **milk**
50g 2oz **butter**
30ml 2tbsp **plain flour**
salt and pepper
15ml 1tbsp **French mustard**
1 small **onion**, peeled and quartered
50g 2oz **blue cheese**

 Top and tail the leeks and slice into food processor bowl. Cook in boiling salted water for 20 minutes until tender. Drain, reserving 275ml (½ pint) of the liquid.

Grate the cheese and reserve.

Place the milk, reserved stock, butter, flour and salt and pepper into the processor bowl and mix together for 10 seconds. Transfer to a saucepan and bring to the boil stirring all the time.

Add the grated cheese and mustard and stir until cheese melts. Season well.

Pour the sauce over the cooked leeks.

Place the onion and blue cheese in the processor bowl and chop finely, sprinkle over the top of the dish and place under a grill to brown topping.

Serve immediately.

Braised Cabbage

2 carrots, peeled
1 small white cabbage, quartered, core removed
2 medium onions, peeled and quartered
100g 4oz streaky bacon
2 cloves of garlic, peeled
25g 1oz butter
15ml 1tbsp oil
salt and pepper

1 Slice the carrots and cabbage into the processor bowl.

Blanch the carrots and cabbage in boiling salted water for 8 minutes. Drain thoroughly.

2 Place the onions, bacon and garlic into the food processor and roughly chop.

Melt the butter and oil in a large frying pan and add the onions, bacon and garlic and fry until the onions become transparent.

Add the strained cabbage and carrots to the remaining ingredients and fry gently for 10 minutes, stirring occasionally.

Season with salt and pepper and transfer into a serving dish.

Garlic Mushrooms

1 medium onion, peeled and quartered
2 garlic cloves, peeled
50g 2oz butter
400g 14oz can tomatoes, drained
bouquet garni
1.5ml ¼tsp oregano
salt and pepper
350g 12oz button mushrooms, washed

1 Place the onion and garlic in the processor bowl and chop finely.

Melt the butter in a saucepan and fry the onion and garlic until browned.

2 Place the tomatoes into the processor bowl and chop finely.

Add the tomatoes, bouquet garni, oregano, salt and pepper to the onions, stirring well.

3 Slice the mushrooms into the processor bowl and add to the prepared ingredients. Cover and simmer for 15 minutes over a low heat.

Serve hot.

Ratatouille

2 small aubergines
15ml 1tbsp **salt**
1 large onion, peeled and quartered
1 green pepper, de-seeded
1 red pepper, de-seeded
3 courgettes
45ml 3tbsp **oil**
1 garlic clove, peeled and crushed
400g 14oz **can tomatoes**
30ml 2tbsp **tomato purée**
salt and freshly ground pepper

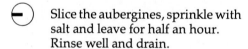

Slice the aubergines, sprinkle with salt and leave for half an hour. Rinse well and drain.

Slice the onion, green and red peppers and courgettes. Heat the oil in a large pan, and fry the sliced onion, garlic and peppers for 10 minutes.

Add the aubergines, courgettes, tomatoes and tomato purée and cover and simmer for 30 minutes. Season to taste.

Serve hot or cold with French bread.

Savoury Stuffed Tomatoes

8 medium tomatoes
75g 3oz **Cheddar cheese, cubed**
25g 1oz **walnuts**
4 spring onions, halved
1 garlic clove
75g 3oz **button mushrooms**
25g 1oz **butter**
15ml 1tbsp **Worcestershire sauce**
salt and pepper
parsley sprigs and lettuce leaves to garnish

Cut the tops off the tomatoes. Scoop out the core and seeds.

Place the Cheddar cheese and walnuts in the processor bowl and chop finely. Reserve.

Place the onions, garlic and mushrooms in the processor bowl and chop finely.

Heat the butter in a pan and fry the chopped onion and mushrooms until soft. Remove from heat.

Stir in the cheese, walnuts, Worcestershire sauce and seasoning.

Spoon the mixture into the tomato shells, stand in bun tins and cook at 200°C, 400°F, Gas No. 6 for 15 minutes.

Stand on lettuce leaves and garnish with parsley sprigs to serve.

Fennel & Cheese Salad

1 medium onion, peeled and quartered
1 large bulb fennel
1 cos lettuce
100g 4oz stilton cheese
60ml 4tbsp olive oil
15ml 1tbsp lemon juice
pinch dried marjoram
salt and pepper

Place the onion in the processor bowl and chop finely. Transfer into a large bowl.

Slice the fennel and lettuce, and add to the chopped onion. Mix well.

Grate the cheese and mix together with the fennel, lettuce and onion.

Beat together the oil, lemon juice, marjoram and salt and pepper.

Pour salad dressing over the salad and toss together well. Serve immediately.

Curried Rice Salad

100g 4oz boiled, cooled rice
2 fresh peaches, peeled, stones removed
1 tomato
1 green pepper, de-seeded
1 red pepper, de-seeded
1 small onion, peeled and quartered
2.5ml ½tsp curry powder
30ml 2tbsp mayonnaise
15ml 1tbsp chutney
salt and pepper
parsley to garnish

Place the cooked rice in a large serving bowl.

Put the peaches, tomato, green and red pepper into the processor bowl and roughly chop.

Place the onion in the processor bowl and chop finely. Add to the other prepared ingredients.

Mix together the curry powder, mayonnaise, chutney, salt and pepper. Add to the prepared ingredients and mix together well.

Garnish with chopped parsley.

Midweek Salad

3 sticks washed celery, cut into pieces
50g 2oz **walnuts**
2 dessert apples, peeled and cored
350g 12oz **garlic sausage**
50g 2oz **sultanas**
60ml 4tbsp **olive oil**
30ml 2tbsp **lemon juice**
salt and ground black pepper
one third cucumber

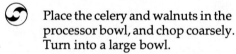 Place the celery and walnuts in the processor bowl, and chop coarsely. Turn into a large bowl.

Grate the apples and add to the chopped celery and walnuts.

Cut the garlic sausage into strips, or slice using the slicing attachment to your processor, and add to the salad ingredients, together with the sultanas.

Mix the olive oil and lemon juice together, season and pour onto the salad. Toss together.

Arrange the salad on a plate.

Using the processor slice the cucumber and arrange on the salad dish.

Bavarian Salad

50g 2oz **walnuts**
½ **small red cabbage**
4 sticks washed celery
2 medium carrots
90ml 6tbsp **Mayonnaise**
90ml 6tbsp **lemon juice**
salt and pepper
chopped parsley for garnish

Place the walnuts in the processor bowl and coarsely chop. Remove and reserve.

Change to the slicing disc and slice the cabbage and celery.

Using the grating disc, grate the carrots and add to the walnuts, cabbage and celery salad.

Add the mayonnaise, lemon juice and seasoning and mix thoroughly.

Sprinkle with parsley before serving.

Sweet Chicken Coleslaw

200g 8oz **white cabbage**
1 large onion, peeled and halved
3 large carrots
300g 12oz **cooked chicken, diced**
50g 2oz **raisins**
120ml 8tbsp **mayonnaise**
5ml 1tsp **salt**
freshly ground black pepper.

 Slice the white cabbage and onion and turn into a mixing bowl.

 Grate the carrots and mix with the cabbage and onion.

Add the chicken pieces and raisins.

Add mayonnaise, salt and ground black pepper to taste, toss well and serve immediately.

Party Salad Wheel

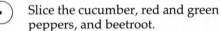

200g 8oz **carrots**
½ **cucumber**
1 green pepper, de-seeded
1 red pepper, de-seeded
200g 8oz **cooked beetroot**

 Grate the carrots.

Slice the cucumber, red and green peppers, and beetroot.

Arrange the salad on a large round tray, or platter. Begin by placing the cucumber slices around the outside edge. Make a circle of the beetroot, then a circle of grated carrot.

Mix the red and green pepper slices together and arrange in the centre.

Serve with garlic and parsley mayonnaise.

Supper Snacks

Egg & Tuna Pickups

200g 8oz **plain flour**
pinch salt
50g 2oz **butter, cubed**
50g 2oz **lard, cubed**
45-60ml 3-4tbsp **water**
2 size 3 **eggs, hard-boiled and halved**
98g 3½oz **can tuna fish, drained**
15ml 1tbsp **tomato ketchup**
15ml 1tbsp **lemon juice**
salt and pepper

 For the pastry, place the flour, salt and fats in the processor bowl and process until the mixture resembles fine breadcrumbs.

Add the water slowly through the feed chute and process to a firm dough. Chill.

Place the eggs, tuna fish, tomato ketchup, lemon juice and seasoning in the processor bowl and process until all the ingredients are combined.

Roll out the pastry to a 30 x 23cm (12" x 9") oblong and cut into twelve 7.5cm (3") squares.

Place a little mixture in the centre of each, dampen edges, fold over to form a triangle and seal edges. Bake in the oven 200°C, 400°F, Gas No. 6 for 25 minutes, until the pastry is golden.

Hawaiian Bacon Burgers

25g 1oz **crustless white bread**
1 **small onion, peeled and quartered**
150g 6oz **streaky bacon, derinded and diced**
150g 6oz **stewing steak, cubed**
salt and pepper
4 **pineapple rings**
100g 4oz **Cheddar cheese, grated**
4 **soft baps, halved and toasted**

 Break the bread into pieces, place in the processor bowl and chop finely.

Add the onion, streaky bacon, cubed stewing steak and salt and pepper, and chop coarsely.

Turn the mixture onto floured board, divide into four and shape into rounds.

Place the burgers under a moderate grill and cook for about 10 minutes, turning once.

Place a pineapple ring on top of each burger, sprinkle cheese on top and grill for a few minutes.

Place the burgers in split baps and serve with salad and pickles.

Country Vegetable Omlette

1 small onion, peeled and quartered
½ green pepper, de-seeded and cut into 4
15ml 1tbsp oil
50g 2oz button mushrooms
2 tomatoes sliced
4 size 3 eggs
salt and ground black pepper

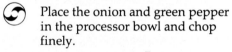 Place the onion and green pepper in the processor bowl and chop finely.

Heat the oil in a 20-23cm (8-9 inches) frying pan and fry the chopped onion and pepper until soft.

Slice the mushrooms and add to the onion mixture. Fry for a further 2 minutes.

Add the tomatoes.

Break the eggs in the processor bowl, season, beat and whisk. Pour into the pan.

Fry the omelette until set, 5-8 minutes, and serve immediately.

Macaroni with Bacon Sauce

200g 8oz macaroni
1 onion, peeled and quartered
4 sticks celery, washed
200g 8oz streaky bacon, derinded and diced
15ml 1tbsp oil
25g 1oz plain flour
500ml 1 pint milk
salt and pepper

Cook the macaroni in boiling salted water for 20 minutes. Drain.

Meanwhile, slice the onion and celery, and reserve.

Place the streaky bacon in the processor bowl and chop finely.

Heat the oil in a pan and fry the onion, celery and bacon together until soft. Stir in flour.

Remove from the heat and gradually stir in the milk.

Return to the heat and bring to the boil, stirring until the sauce thickens. Season to taste.

Place the macaroni in a serving dish and cover with the bacon sauce.

Cheddarburgers

50g 2oz **crustless white bread**
1 small onion, **peeled and quartered**
100g 4oz **Cheddar cheese, cubed**
350g 12oz **stewing beef, diced**
5ml 1tsp **salt**
freshly ground black pepper
1 size 3 egg
4 soft baps
tomato and cucumber to garnish

 Break the bread into pieces and place in processor bowl and chop finely.

Add the onion, cheese and meat and chop coarsely.

Add the seasoning and egg and process until combined.

Shape into four burgers and cook under a hot grill for 15 minutes, turning once.

Split each bap and fill with a Cheddarburger. Garnish with tomato and cucumber slices and serve.

Curried Beef Pasties

200g 8oz **stewing steak, diced**
1 medium onion, **peeled and quartered**
1 medium potato, **peeled and quartered**
10ml 2tsp **curry powder**
15ml 1tbsp **oil**
salt and pepper
350g 12oz **plain flour**
175g 6oz **hard margarine**
pinch of salt
water to mix
beaten egg to glaze

 Place the diced stewing steak, onion, potato and curry powder in the processor bowl and process until coarsely chopped.

Heat the oil and fry the meat mixture gently for 15 minutes. Season and allow to cool.

Make pastry following the instructions on page 7. Roll out, cut into 15cm (6 inches) rounds.

Place the meat mixture in the centre of each pastry round, dampen edges, and pinch to seal. Flute the edges.

Place on a baking sheet, brush with beaten egg and bake at 210°C, 425°F, Gas No. 7 for 20-25 minutes, until golden.

Quick Pan Pizza

150g 6oz **self-raising flour**
pinch of salt
2.5ml ½tsp **baking powder**
50g 2oz **margarine, diced**
90ml 6tbsp **milk**
75g 3oz **Cheddar cheese**
1 large onion, peeled and cut into 8
396g 14oz **can tomatoes**
salt and pepper
4 frankfurters, cut in half lengthways

 Place the flour, salt, margarine and baking powder in the processor bowl and chop finely.

Add the milk and process to a soft dough. Roll into 25cm (10") round.

Press the dough into a greased 25cm (10") frying pan, cover and cook over a low heat for 10-15 minutes, until golden.

 Grate the cheese and set aside.

 Place the onion in the processor bowl and chop finely.

Put the chopped onion in saucepan with tomatoes and boil until thickened and reduced by half. Season.

Spread on the dough, arrange the frankfurters on top, and sprinkle with cheese.

Cook under a hot grill for 4 minutes.

Cheesy Chicken Balls

25g 1oz **butter**
25g 1oz **flour**
150ml ¼ pint **milk**
salt and pepper
150g 6oz **crustless white bread**
200g 8oz **cooked chicken**
75g 3oz **Cheddar cheese**
1 size 3 egg
oil for frying

Melt the butter in a pan and stir in the flour. Add the milk gradually, stirring until thickened. Season and allow to cool.

 Break the bread into pieces, place in processor bowl and chop finely. Reserve half the crumbs.

Add the cooked chicken and cheese to half the crumbs in the processor bowl, and chop finely.

Add the sauce and egg to the bowl and process until smooth.

Roll the mixture into 16 balls and coat in the remaining crumbs.

Heat the oil and deep fry the cheesy chicken balls until golden, 1 minute. Drain.

Put a cocktail stick through each and serve hot or cold.

Portuguese Toasts

6 parsley sprigs
1 garlic clove, peeled
113g 4oz **carton cottage cheese**
113g 4oz **carton cream cheese**
129g 4½oz **can sardines in tomato sauce**
15ml 1tbs **Worcestershire sauce**
salt and pepper
4 slices toast, buttered
4 lemon slices to garnish

 Place the parsley sprigs in the processor bowl, and chop coarsely.

Reserve 15ml (1tbsp) of parsley to garnish.

Place the cottage cheese in processor bowl and process until all ingredients are combined.

Spread mixture onto 4 pieces of toast and cook under moderate grill until just beginning to brown. Sprinkle reserved parsley on top and finish with a twist of lemon on each.

Chicken Loaf

1 large onion, peeled and cut into 8
1 garlic clove, peeled
100g 4oz **streaky bacon, derinded and diced**
25g 1oz **butter**
198g 7oz **can sweetcorn kernels**
350g 12oz **cooked chicken, diced**
1 small bloomer loaf
149g 5oz **can condensed mushroom soup**

 Place the onion, garlic and streaky bacon in the processor bowl and chop coarsely.

Melt the butter in a frying pan, add the chopped ingredients and fry for 10 minutes. Leave to cool slightly.

Add the sweetcorn and diced chicken.

 Cut a horizontal slice across the top of the loaf and scoop out the bread from the inside. Use 75g (3oz) of the bread, place in processor bowl and chop finely.

Mix the breadcrumbs and chicken mixture together with the soup.

Spoon mixture into the loaf shell pressing it well down. Replace top.

Wrap in foil and bake at 200°C, 400°F, Gas No. 6 for 30 minutes.

Savoury Cheese Crunch

100g 4oz **crustless brown or white bread**
1 large onion, peeled and quartered
100g 4oz **mushrooms**
15ml 1tbsp **oil**
6 hard boiled eggs, halved
100g 4oz **Cheddar cheese**
298g 10½oz **can condensed celery soup**

Break the bread into pieces, place in the processor bowl, chop finely and put to one side.

Slice the onion and mushrooms.

Heat the oil, fry the sliced onion and mushrooms until soft, then transfer to a a 1·2 litre (2 pint) ovenproof dish.

Roughly chop the hard boiled eggs and add to the dish.

Grate the cheese and sprinkle over the egg.

Gently warm the condensed celery soup and spoon over the cheese.

Cover the dish with the breadcrumbs and bake at 190°C, 375°F, Gas No. 5 for 30 minutes.

Caribbean Grill

4 gammon picnic steaks
75g 3oz **crustless white bread**
6 pineapple rings
15ml 1tbsp **clear honey**
salt and pepper

Cook the gammon steaks under a medium grill for 3-5 minutes. Turn.

Break the bread into pieces, place in the processor bowl and chop finely.

Add two pineapple rings and chop finely.

Add the honey and seasoning and process to combine all the ingredients.

Spoon the mixture onto the gammon steaks and return to the grill. Cook for 10 minutes until the breadcrumbs are crispy.

Cut the remaining pineapple rings into four pieces, and place on top of the gammon steaks to garnish.

Mushroom & Courgette Flan

150g 6oz **flour**
pinch of salt
75g 3oz **hard margarine**
water to mix
1 medium **onion, peeled and quartered**
100g 4oz **button mushrooms**
100g 4oz **courgettes**
50g 2oz **Cheddar cheese**
25g 1oz **butter**
2 size 3 **eggs**
250ml ½ pint **milk**
salt and pepper

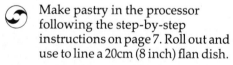 Make pastry in the processor following the step-by-step instructions on page 7. Roll out and use to line a 20cm (8 inch) flan dish.

Slice the onion, mushrooms, courgettes and cheese.

Heat the butter in a pan. Add the onions and fry until soft.

Place the onions, mushrooms and courgettes into pastry case and place the cheese slices on top.

Beat together the eggs, milk and seasoning and pour into the flan case.

Bake at 180°C, 350°F, Gas No. 4 for 30 minutes until browned.

Sausage & Apple Patties

1 small **onion, peeled and quartered**
1 dessert **apple, peeled and cored**
350g 12oz **pork sausagemeat**
5ml 1tsp **mixed herbs**
45ml 3tbsp **tomato ketchup**
2.5ml ½tsp **salt**
ground black pepper
4 size 3 **eggs**

Place the onion and apple in the processor bowl and chop finely. Add the pork sausagemeat, mixed herbs and seasoning, and process until the mixture is smooth.

Shape into four flattened rounds and cook under a hot grill for 15 minutes, turning once.

Top each pattie with a fried egg to serve.

Sauces & Dressings

Mayonnaise

1 size 3 **egg yolk**
1 size 3 **egg**
2.5ml ½tsp **dry mustard**
salt and pepper
250ml ½ pint **salad oil**
15ml 1tbsp **wine vinegar**

Place egg yolk and egg, mustard, salt and pepper in to the processor bowl.

Process together for 5 seconds.

With the machine running gradually add the oil until the mayonnaise is thick and creamy. At first add the oil drip by drip as too quick an addition of oil can curdle the mayonnaise. As the mayonnaise begins to thicken the oil can be added at a quicker rate.

Finally, add the vinegar.

Variations:
Garlic & Parsley Mayonnaise:
Chop 1-2 garlic cloves in processor bowl and add 8 large parsley sprigs. Stir into the basic Mayonnaise.

Tartare Sauce: Place 25g (1oz) gherkins, 50g (2oz) pickled onions and 25g (1oz) capers in processor bowl and chop finely. Stir into the basic Mayonnaise.

Apple Sauce

450g 1lb **cooking apples, peeled and cored**
4 **cloves**
45ml 3tbsp **water**
pinch salt
10ml 2tsp **brown sugar**
25g 1oz **butter**

Slice the apples into the processor bowl.

Put the sliced apple and cloves into a saucepan with the water and cook until soft. Remove cloves.

Return the cooked apple to the processor bowl and add the salt, sugar and butter and blend well together.

Serve hot or cold, or as an accompaniment to pork, duck and goose dishes.

Bread Sauce

2 small onions, peeled
2 cloves of garlic
bouquet garni
275ml ½ pint milk
50g 2oz white bread, cubed
25g 1oz butter
30ml 2tbsp single cream
salt and pepper

Press a garlic clove into the centre of each onion and place in a saucepan.

Add the bouquet garni and milk and bring to the boil. Cover and simmer for 10 minutes.

 Chop the bread into breadcrumbs.

Strain the liquid ingredients and with the food processor running, add the warm liquid down through the feeder chute with the butter and cream.

Mix together well and season with salt and pepper.

Serve hot as an accompaniment to chicken.

Parsley Sauce

25g 1oz fresh parsley, stalks removed
25g 1oz butter
25g 1oz flour
275ml ½ pint milk
salt and pepper

 Place the parsley in the processor bowl and chop finely.

To the parsley in the bowl add the butter, flour and milk and process together for 5 seconds.

Pour sauce into a saucepan and bring to the boil stirring continuously. Cook for a further 2 minutes.

Season to taste and serve as an accompaniment to gammon or vegetables.

Cheese Sauce

100g 4oz **strong cheddar cheese**
25g 1oz **butter, softened**
25g 1oz **plain flour**
275ml ½pt **milk**
2.5ml ½tsp **English mustard**
5ml 1tsp **Worcestershire sauce**
salt and pepper

 Grate the cheese into the food processor bowl and reserve.

 Put the butter, flour and milk into the processor bowl and mix together for 5 seconds.

Pour the liquid into a saucepan, bring to the boil, stirring all the time, and cook for 2 minutes.

Remove from the heat and stir in the cheese, mustard, Worcestershire sauce and seasoning.

Serve as an accompaniment to fish or vegetables.

Blue Cheese Dressing

1 small onion, peeled and quartered
50g 2oz **blue cheese**
150ml 5fl oz **carton soured cream**
30ml 2tbsp **top of the milk**
salt and pepper

 Place the onion into the processor bowl and chop finely.

Add the blue cheese, sour cream, milk and seasoning and mix together for 10 seconds.

Adjust seasoning if required and if a thinner dressing is preferred add a little more milk.

Serve with green or mixed salad.

Desserts

Peach & Chocolate Layer

200g 8oz **chocolate digestive biscuits**
411g 14½oz **can sliced peaches, drained**
275ml ½ pint **thick sweetened custard**
2.5ml ½tsp **grated lemon rind**

 Place the biscuits in the processor bowl and chop finely.

Reserve 4 peach slices. Place the remaining peaches, custard and lemon rind into the processor bowl and process until smooth.

Place one third of the biscuit crumbs into the bottom of 4 individual glass dishes.

Divide half of the fruit between the dishes.

Repeat the process again with crumbs then fruit, finishing with a layer of crumbs on top.

Decorate each glass dish with a peach slice.

Raspberry Soufflé

15ml 1tbsp **gelatine**
45ml 3tbsp **hot water**
150ml ¼ pint **fresh raspberries**
10ml 2tsp **lemon juice**
50g 2oz **icing sugar, sifted**
2 size 3 **egg whites**
150ml ¼ pint **double cream**

Note *For variable speed food processors only*

Prepare a ½ litre, (1 pint) souffle dish by putting a 10cm (4″) strip of greaseproof paper around the dish, making sure the paper stands 4-5cm (1½″-2″) above the edge of the dish. Tie on securely with string.

Put the gelatine and hot water in a basin and stir over a pan of boiling water until dissolved.

 Purée the raspberries on a low speed, and with the machine still running, add the lemon juice, dissolved gelatine and icing sugar. Turn out into a bowl and reserve.

 Whisk egg whites to a stiff snow and turn out into a bowl, reserve.

Whisk the cream to a soft piping consistency.

On a low speed add the whisked egg whites and raspberry purée to the whipped cream, and gently fold everything together.

Pour into the prepared soufflé dish. The mixture should reach almost to the top of the paper.

Chill until firm and set. Just before serving ease paper away from the mixture with a knife dipped in hot water.

Decorate with whipped cream and whole raspberries.

Walnut Ice Cream

275ml ½ pint **double cream**
150ml ¼ pint **single cream**
75g 3oz **icing sugar, sieved**
100g 4oz **crustless brown bread**
100g 4oz **walnuts**
15ml 1tbsp **rum**
2 size 3 eggs, separated

Place the double cream into the processor bowl and whisk until just stiff. If you have a variable speed food processor gradually increase the speed to prevent the cream splashing up the sides of the bowl.

Whisk in the single cream and then gently fold in the icing sugar. Reserve

Break the bread into pieces and place in the processor bowl. Process for 10 seconds, until a fine breadcrumb stage.

Add the nuts to the breadcrumbs and chop finely. Gently fold the crumbs and nuts into the cream mixture.

Mix together the rum and egg yolks and fold in to the mixture. Reserve.

Whisk egg whites until almost stiff, add all the ingredients to the egg whites and gently mix together.

Pour into freezing trays and freeze until firm. Serve with biscuits.

Strawberry Cloud

25g 1oz **blanched almonds**
50g 2oz **butter**
150ml ¼ pint **water**
65g 2½oz **plain flour**
pinch of salt
2 size 3 eggs, beaten
275ml ½ pint **double cream, whipped**
40g 1½oz **icing sugar, sieved**
15ml 1tbsp **brandy (optional)**
200g 8oz **strawberries**

 Place the almonds in the processor bowl and chop finely. Reserve.

In a saucepan melt the butter in the water and bring to the boil, then remove from the heat.

 Add the flour and the salt and cook for 2 minutes. Return mixture to the processor bowl. Add the eggs and process for 1 minute, until the mixture has a nice sheen.

Spoon the mixture onto a greased baking tray in a 20cm (8 inch) ring and sprinkle with almonds.

Bake at 220°C, 425°F, Gas No. 7 for 30 minutes in the centre of the oven.

Place on a wire cooling rack and allow to cool. Split in half horizontally.

 Place the cream, icing sugar and brandy into the processor bowl and blend together well for 10 seconds. Reserve.

Slice the strawberries and fold into cream. Use to fill the choux ring.

Pashka

500g 1lb **cream cheese**
100g 4oz **butter, softened**
125g 5oz **caster sugar**
142ml 5fl oz **carton soured cream**
50g 2oz **glacé cherries, washed**
150g 6oz **blanched whole almonds**
50g 2oz **mixed peel**
200g 8oz **raisins**

 Place the cheese, butter, sugar, soured cream and cherries in the processor bowl and process until smooth.

Fold in the nuts, peel and raisins.

Spoon mixture into a dampened 1·4 litre (2½ pint) deep ring mould. Cover with greaseproof paper and weights.

Chill overnight until firm.

To serve, partially immerse the mould in a bowl of hot water. Run a knife around the edge and turn onto a serving plate.

Chill for 1 hour.

Decorate with whipped cream and cherries and angelica if required.

Honey & Hazelnut Cheesecake

150g 6oz **digestive biscuits, broken**
75g 3oz **butter, melted**
15g ½oz **powdered gelatine**
30ml 2tbsp **water**
100g 4oz **hazelnuts**
200g 8oz **cream cheese**
60ml 4tbsp **honey**
2 size 3 eggs, separated
250ml ½ pint **double cream**
whole hazelnuts to decorate

Place the biscuits in the processor bowl and chop finely.

Add the melted butter and press over the base of a 9" loose bottomed tin. Chill.

Dissolve the gelatine in water over a bowl of hot water.

Place the hazelnuts in the processor bowl and process until finely chopped.

Add the cream cheese, honey and egg yolks and process together for 5 seconds.

Turn into a large bowl.

Whisk the egg whites until stiff. Reserve.

Whisk the cream until thick. Add the creamed cheese mixture, gelatine and egg whites to the cream and mix together well. Pour over base and chill until set.

Remove from tin and decorate with cream and hazelnuts.

Apple & Lemon Pudding

1 medium cooking apple, peeled and cored
150g 6oz **self-raising flour**
5ml 1tsp **baking powder**
2.5ml ½tsp **salt**
1.25ml ¼tsp **cinnamon**
grated rind of 1 lemon
150g 6oz **soft margarine**
150g 6oz **caster sugar**
3 size 3 eggs
75g 3oz **currants**

 Place the apple in the processor bowl and chop finely. Reserve.

 Place the flour, baking powder, salt and cinnamon into the processor bowl and mix together for 5 seconds.

Add all the remaining ingredients, except the currants to the dry ingredients in the processor bowl.

Process for 30 seconds until light and creamy.

Stir in the currants and chopped apple.

Spoon into a greased 1·4 litres (2½ pint) pudding basin and cover tightly with greased foil.

Steam for 2-2½ hours.

Serve with golden syrup.

Black Forest Gâteau

125g 5oz **self raising flour**
25g 1oz **cocoa**
7.5ml 1½tsp **baking powder**
150g 6oz **butter**
3 size 3 **eggs**
150g 6oz **caster sugar**
90ml 6tbsp **cherry jam**
100g 4oz **plain chocolate**
150ml ¼ pint **double cream, whipped**
425g 15oz **can black cherries**
10ml 2tsp **arrowroot**

 Place the flour, cocoa, baking powder, butter, eggs and caster sugar into the processor bowl and process for 20 seconds until light and fluffy. After 10 seconds stop the machine and scrape down ingredients.

Divide the mixture between 2 greased 7" sandwich tins.

Bake in the centre of the oven at 180°C, 350°F, Gas No. 4 for 25-30 minutes. After 5 minutes turn out onto a wire cooling rack and cool.

Sandwich together with some of the jam. Spread the sides with the rest of the jam.

 Using the processor, grate the chocolate. Use to cover the sides.

Pipe the whipped cream around the top of the cake.

Drain cherries and place on the cake.

Mix the arrowroot with a little of the cherry juice. Heat rest of juice in a saucepan and bring to the boil and glaze cherries.

Treacle Tart

150g 6oz **plain flour**
pinch salt
75g 3oz **hard margarine**
water to mix
90ml 6tbsp **golden syrup**
30ml 2tbsp **black treacle**
30ml 2tbsp **lemon juice**
50g 2oz **crustless white bread**
milk to glaze

 Place the flour, salt and margarine into the processor bowl and process together for 10 seconds (breadcrumb stage).

With the machine running slowly add the water down through the feed chute, until the mixture starts to form little tiny balls. At this stage stop adding the water and allow the food processor to continue mixing until a dough ball is formed.

Roll out the pastry and use to line a 20cm (8 inch) flan dish or pie plate, reserving trimmings.

Warm the syrup, treacle and lemon juice in a saucepan.

 Break the bread into pieces, place in the processor bowl and chop finely into breadcrumbs.

Add the warm syrup to the breadcrumbs and mix together well. Pour into the pastry case. Roll out the pastry trimmings, cut into long strips and arrange in a lattice design on the tart. Brush pastry with milk.

Bake in the centre of the oven at 200°C, 400°F, Gas No. 6 for 20-30 minutes.

Cordon Bleu Cake

200g 7oz **butter, softened**	30 **Nice biscuits**
100g 4oz **caster sugar**	**cherries to decorate**
200g 7oz **cream cheese**	60ml 4tbsp **caster sugar**
1 size 3 **egg**	60ml 4tbsp **water**
5ml 1tsp **lemon juice**	30ml 2tbsp **cocoa**
2.5ml ½tsp **cinammon**	100g 4oz **plain chocolate**
90ml 6tbsp **brandy**	100g 4oz **almonds for decoration**
90ml 6tbsp **milk**	

 Cream the butter and sugar together until light and fluffy, stopping the food processor during creaming to scrape down the ingredients.

Add the cream cheese, egg, lemon juice and cinammon and mix together well.

Mix the brandy and milk together in a basin.

Lay out a large piece of foil on a flat surface.

Dip the biscuits in the brandy mixture and lay them on the foil 3 biscuits wide x 5 biscuits lengthwise.

Spread a thin layer of the cheesy mixture on top of the biscuits.

Dip the remaining biscuits in the brandy mix and lay them on top of the spread.

Spread the remaining mixture down the centre row of the biscuits. Place a row of cherries down the centre.

Pull up the foil sides lightly to make the cake into a triangle shape. Refrigerate overnight.

In a saucepan boil the sugar, water, cocoa and chocolate for 2 minutes.

Remove from the heat and beat in the butter. Cool slightly.

Remove the foil from the cake and place on a serving dish. Brush the melted chocolate over the biscuit mixture and sprinkle with the flaked almonds. Refrigerate.

Golden Fruit Pie

500g 1lb **firm pears, peeled and cored**
500g 1lb **cooking apples, peeled and cored**
30ml 2tbsp **clear honey**
30ml 2tbsp **lemon juice**
15ml 1tbsp **cornflour**
15ml 1tbsp **water**
250g 10oz **plain flour**
125g 5oz **hard margarine**
pinch salt
water to mix
1 size 3 egg white
25g 1oz **caster sugar**

Slice the apples and the pears.

Place in a saucepan with the honey and lemon juice.

Cook for 10 minutes until soft.

Blend the cornflour with the water and add to the fruit. Stir until thickened then cool.

Place the flour, salt and margarine in the processor bowl and process for 10 seconds until the mixture resembles breadcrumbs.

With the machine running, slowly add the water down the feed chute, until the mixture starts to form into little balls.

At this stage stop adding the water and allow the processor to continue mixing until a dough ball is formed.

Divide the pastry in half. Roll out one half to cover a 23cm (9 inch) pie plate and place the filling on top of the pastry. Roll out the remaining pastry and use to cover the pie. Seal edges. Brush the top well with egg white and sprinkle with caster sugar.

Bake in the centre of the oven at 200°C, 400°F, Gas No. 6 for 30 minutes until golden brown.

Christmas Pudding

225g 8oz **white bread, crusts removed**
100g 4oz **plain flour, sifted**
2.5ml ½tsp **mixed spice**
2.5ml ½tsp **nutmeg**
275g 10oz **shredded suet**
225g 8oz **dark brown sugar**
700g 1½lbs **mixed fruit**
50g 2oz **mixed peel**
50g 2oz **glace cherries**
50g 2oz **flaked almonds**
grated rind of 1 orange and 1 lemon
4 size 3 eggs
75ml 3fl oz **sherry**
150ml 5fl oz **milk**

 Place the bread into the processor bowl and process for 10 seconds to the breadcrumb stage.

 Add all the dry ingredients to the breadcrumbs and process for 20 seconds.

With the food processor running continuously, add the eggs, sherry and milk and mix together until well combined.

Turn out into a buttered 1½ litre (2½ pint) pudding basin. Cover with buttered greaseproof paper and steam for 6 hours.

Turn out and leave to cool and then wrap in greaseproof paper and aluminium foil. Store until needed.

Return to buttered pudding basin and steam for a further 2 hours when needed.

Pineapple & Lemon Mousse

40g 1½oz **toasted almonds**
3 size 3 eggs, separated
75g 3oz **caster sugar**
grated rind and juice of 1 lemon
15g ½oz **powdered gelatine**
30ml 2tbsp **water**
226g 8oz **can pineapple slices, drained**
150ml ¼ pint **double cream, lightly whipped**

 Place the almonds in the processor bowl, chop finely and reserve.

Put egg yolks, sugar, lemon rind and juice into a bowl over hot water and whisk until thick and creamy.

Dissolve the gelatine in the water.

 Reserve one pineapple slice. Chop the rest in the processor and fold into the mixture.

Stir in the gelatine and fold in almost all the cream, reserving a little for decoration.

 Whisk the egg whites and fold into the mixture.

Pour the mousse into a serving dish and chill to set.

Decorate the top with chopped almonds, the remaining cream and pineapple slice.

Ribboned Trifle

150g 6oz **crustless white bread**
50g 2oz **butter**
25g 1oz **demerara sugar**
300g 12oz **cooking apples, peeled and cored**
25g 1oz **sugar**
219g 7¾oz **can blackberries**
250ml ½ pint **double cream**
15ml 1tbsp **icing sugar**
30ml 2tbsp **lemon juice**

 Break bread into pieces, place in the processor bowl and chop finely.

Melt the butter in a pan and fry the crumbs until golden and crisp.

Allow to cool and stir in the demerara sugar.

─ Slice the apples in the processor and cook with the sugar until soft.

 Process the apple to a purée and stir in the blackberries and juice.

 Whisk the cream, icing sugar and lemon juice until just stiff.

Place the fruit in the bottom of a 0·5 litre (1 pint) glass dish. Cover with nearly all the cream. Top with the breadcrumb mixture and decorate with remaining cream.

Orange & Coffee Gâteau

150g 6oz **self-raising flour**
7.5ml 1½tsp **baking powder**
30ml 2tbsp **coffee essence**
150g 6oz **soft margarine**
3 size 3 eggs
150g 6oz **caster sugar**
100g 4oz **walnuts**
150g 6oz **butter, softened**
300g 12oz **icing sugar, sieved**
5ml 1tsp **finely grated orange rind**
312g 11oz **can mandarins, drained**

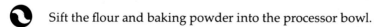 Sift the flour and baking powder into the processor bowl.

Add the coffee essence, margarine, eggs and caster sugar and process for 20 seconds. After 10 seconds stop the machine and scrape down the ingredients.

Pour into a greased 23cm (9 inch) square cake tin and bake at 180°C, 350°F, Gas No. 4 for 40-45 minutes.

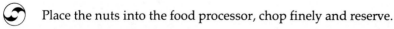 Place the nuts into the food processor, chop finely and reserve.

Place the butter, icing sugar and orange rind together into the processor bowl and mix together well.

Split cake in half and sandwich together with two thirds of the butter icing.

Ice cake all over with remaining butter icing and coat sides in chopped nuts.

Pipe the rest of the icing on the cake and decorate with the mandarins.

Chocolate & Banana Pudding

2 ripe bananas
100g 4oz **self-raising flour**
5ml 1tsp **baking powder**
15ml 1tbsp **cocoa powder**
100g 4oz **soft margarine**
100g 4oz **caster sugar**
2 size 3 eggs
100g 4oz **plain chocolate**
25g 1oz **butter**
30ml 2tbsp **milk**

 Using the processor slice bananas. Reserve.

 Place the flour, baking powder and cocoa into processor bowl. Add the margarine, sugar and eggs and process for 20 seconds until light and creamy. After 10 seconds stop the machine and scrape down ingredients.

Stir in sliced bananas.

Spoon the mixture into a greased 0·8 litre (1½ pint) fluted mould or ovenproof pudding basin.

Cover tightly with greased foil.

Bake ingredients at 180°C, 350°F, Gas No. 4 for 1 hour in the centre of the oven.

For the sauce, melt the chocolate and the butter in a basin standing in a pan of hot water. Stir in the milk and allow to heat through.

Serve with the pudding.

Bread, Cakes
& Biscuits

White & Wholemeal Bread

15g ½oz **fresh yeast**
5ml 1tsp **caster sugar**
275ml ½ pint **warm water**
either
450g 1lb **strong plain flour**
or
225g 8oz **each of strong plain flour and wholemeal flour**
10ml 2tsp **salt**
25g 1oz **butter**
beaten egg to glaze

In a small bowl cream the fresh yeast with the sugar and warm water to a smooth creamy liquid.

Place the flour and salt in the processor bowl. Add the butter and process for 5 seconds to the breadcrumbed stage.

With the processor running, pour the liquid yeast down the feed chute. As soon as a dough is formed, stop the food processor and remove it.

Using floured hands, shape the dough into a ball and place in an oiled polythene bag.

Leave in a warm place until the dough has doubled in size. Return the dough to the processor bowl and mix for a further 30 seconds.

Shape dough into an oblong and place into a greased 450g (1lb) loaf tin.

Return to the oiled polythene bag and leave to rise again until double in size. Brush top with beaten egg.

Bake in the centre of the oven at 220°C, 425°F, Gas No. 7, for about 30 minutes, until loaf shrinks slightly from the sides.

Cool loaf on a wire cooling rack.

Malt Loaf

75g 3oz **malt extract**
30ml 2tbsp **black treacle**
25g 1oz **butter**
450g 1lb **plain flour, sifted**
5ml 1tsp **salt**
225g 8oz **sultanas**
25g 1oz **fresh yeast (or** 15ml 1tbsp **dried yeast)**
175ml 6fl oz **warm milk**
25g 1oz **caster sugar**

Put the malt extract, treacle and butter into a saucepan and heat gently. Allow to cool.

Put the flour, salt and sultanas into the processor bowl and mix together for 5 seconds.

In a small bowl mix the yeast with the milk and sugar to a smooth creamy liquid.

Add the yeast and malt mixture to the dry ingredients down the feed chute with the machine running until a soft dough is formed.

Turn out onto a lightly floured surface and knead dough lightly until dough is smooth.

Shape to fit a 900g (2lb) greased loaf tin. Place dough in tin and put in a warm spot. Leave to rise until loaf doubles its size.

Bake in the centre of the oven at 200°C, 400°F, Gas No. 6 for 40-45 minutes until a cocktail stick inserted into the centre of the loaf comes out clean.

Turn out onto a wire cooling rack and allow to cool.

Tea Cakes

450g 1lb **plain flour, sifted**
5ml 1tsp **salt**
25g 1oz **butter**
25g 1oz **caster sugar**
50g 2oz **sultanas**
15g ½oz **fresh yeast (or 15ml 1tbsp dried yeast)**
275ml ½ pint **milk**
25g 1oz **caster sugar**
extra milk for brushing

Place the flour, salt and butter in the processor bowl and mix together for 10 seconds.

Add the caster sugar and sultanas and mix together for 5 seconds.

In a small bowl blend the yeast with the warmed milk and sugar to a smooth creamy consistency and leave until frothy.

With the food processor running add all of the liquid ingredients to the dry ingredients down the feed chute and mix to a firm dough.

Turn out onto a lightly floured surface and knead slightly until smooth.

Cover and leave to rise until double in size.

Return dough to food processor bowl and mix for a further 20 seconds. Divide dough into 6 equal size pieces.

Roll each piece into a 15cm (6") round and place on a greased baking tray.

Brush tops with milk and leave to rise until double in size.

Bake in centre of oven at 200°C, 400°F, Gas No. 6 for 20 minutes.

Cut the tea cakes in half, toast, and spread with butter.

Scones

225g 8oz **self raising flour, sifted**
2.5ml ½tsp **salt**
50g 2oz **butter, cubed**
25g 1oz **caster sugar**
125ml 4fl oz **milk**
extra milk for brushing

 Place flour, salt and butter in the processor bowl and process for 10 seconds, until the mixture resembles fine breadcrumbs.

Add the sugar and mix together for 5 seconds.

With the machine still running pour enough milk down through the feeder chute to give a soft dough.

Turn the dough out onto a lightly floured board and roll out into 2cm (¾") thick.

Cut out 12 rounds, using a 5cm (2") cutter. Brush tops with milk.

Place on a greased baking tray and bake in the centre of the oven at 220°C, 425°F, Gas No. 7, for 12 minutes, until golden brown and well-risen.

Cool on a wire cooling rack.

Serve with fresh double cream and strawberries.

Salami & Cheese Scone Round

225g 8oz **self-raising flour**
pinch of salt
50g 2oz **butter, cubed**
50g 2oz **salami, derinded**
75g 3oz **Cheddar cheese, cubed**
75ml 5tbsp **milk**

 Place the flour and salt into the processor bowl with the butter.

Process for 10 seconds until the mixture resembles fine breadcrumbs.

Add the salami and cheese and mix for 10 seconds.

Add the milk and process to a soft dough.

Shape the dough into a flat round, about 20cm (8 inch) in diameter.

Place on a greased baking tray.

Score with a knife into six triangles. Bake in the centre of the oven at 220°C, 425°F, Gas No. 7 for 15 minutes until golden brown.

Serve with a cheese board.

Victoria Sponge

175g 6oz **soft margarine**
175g 6oz **caster sugar**
3 size 3 eggs
225g 8oz **self raising flour**
jam to fill
icing sugar to decorate

Line 2 x 20cm (8 inch) round cake tins with greaseproof paper and grease with butter.

Place the margarine and sugar into the food processor bowl and cream until light and fluffy. During processing stop the machine two or three times and scrape down the mixture.

Beat in the eggs one at a time.

Slowly add the flour down through the feeder chute, mix together until all the flour is incorporated using a pulsing action or low speed.

Transfer to the prepared tins and smooth the tops with a knife.

Naff 160°

Bake in the centre of the oven at 180°C, 350°F, Gas No. 4 for 20-30 minutes, or until a wooden cocktail stick inserted into centre of cake comes out clean.

Leave in the tins for 5 minutes and then turn out onto a wire cooling rack. Carefully peel off greaseproof paper and allow cake to cool.

Spread jam over one half of the cake, and then sandwich the two halves together. Sprinkle the top of the cake with icing sugar.

Swiss Roll

3 size eggs
75g 3oz **caster sugar**
75g 3oz **self raising flour, sifted**
75ml 5tbsp **warmed jam**

Note: *for variable speed food processors only*

Line a 30cm x 20cm (12" x 8") swiss roll tin with greaseproof paper and grease all the surfaces.

 Whisk the eggs and sugar together until the mixture is very light in colour and thick in texture — consistency of softly whipped cream and at least double its volume (approximately 8 minutes).

Select low speed and gently add the sifted flour through the feed chute until all the flour is incorporated.

Transfer to prepared tin and bake towards top of oven, 200°C, 400°F, Gas No. 6 for 10-12 minutes (or until well risen and firm).

Turn out onto a sheet of sugared greaseproof paper and carefully peel off greaseproof paper.

Cut away crisp edges around the swiss roll with a sharp knife.

Spread the jam quickly over the swiss roll and roll up tightly. Hold in position for one minute. Cool on wire rack.

Applecake

175g 6oz **softened butter**
350g 12oz **caster sugar**
3 **size 3 eggs**
350g 12oz **plain flour, sifted**
15ml 1tbsp **baking powder**
45ml 3tbsp **milk**
pinch salt
396g 14oz **tin of apples, drained**
275g 10oz **caster sugar**
90ml 6tbsp **milk**
50g 2oz **butter**

 Cream the butter and caster sugar together in the processor bowl until light and fluffy. Stop the processor two or three times during creaming to scrape down the mixture.

Add the eggs one at a time through the feed chute, with the processor running.

Slowly add the flour, baking powder, milk and salt to the creamed mixture down the feed chute, using either a pulsing action or variable speed. Stop the food processor as soon as the flour is incorporated into the mixture.

Place the cake mixture into a buttered 23cm (9") squared cake tin and arrange the apples on top. Bake at 150°C, 300°F, Gas No. 2 for 1-1¼ hours, until a cocktail stick inserted into centre of cake comes out clean.

Put the sugar, milk and butter into a saucepan and cook for 20 minutes. Pour over warm cake. Serve hot or cold with cream.

Cherry Cobblestone Cake

175g 6oz **soft margarine**
175g 6oz **caster sugar**
3 size 3 **eggs**
100g 4oz **sultanas**
225g 8oz **plain flour**
2.5ml ½tsp **baking powder**
75g 3oz **glacé cherries, quartered**
50g 2oz **glacé cherries, halved**
45ml 3tbsp **apricot jam**
fresh halved cherries to decorate

 Place all the ingredients, except the halved cherries and jam, together in the processor bowl and mix for 30 seconds. After 15 seconds, stop the machine and scrape down the ingredients.

Place in a greased and lined 900g (2lb) loaf tin.

Smooth the top and arrange the halved glacé cherries in rows over the top of the cake.

Bake on the middle shelf of a preheated oven 170°C, 325°F, Gas No. 3 for 2½ hours.

Leave the cake in the tin for a few minutes, then turn out onto a cooling rack.

Place halved fresh cherries over the top of the cake to decorate

In a small saucepan boil the apricot jam and then sieve it. Glaze the top of the cake with the jam.

Mince Pies

100g 4oz **fresh suet**	2.5ml ½tsp **mixed spice**
175g 6oz **cooking apples, peeled and cored**	2.5ml ½tsp **cinnamon**
225g 8oz **raisins**	125ml 4fl oz **brandy**
225g 8oz **currants**	450g 1lb **plain flour, sifted**
100g 4oz **mixed peel**	**pinch of salt**
50g 2oz **blanched almonds**	225g 8oz **hard margarine**
juice and grated rind of 1 lemon	**water to mix**
225g 8oz **soft brown sugar**	**beaten egg to glaze**

 Place the suet into the processor bowl and chop finely. Turn out into a bowl.

Finely chop the apples in the processor bowl.

Return the suet to the food processor with the apples and add all the remaining ingredients. Process together until well mixed. Turn out into a large bowl.

 Place the flour, salt and margarine into the processor bowl and process for 10 seconds until the mixture resembles fine breadcrumbs.

With the machine running, slowly add water down through the feed chute and mix to a soft dough ball.

Turn dough out onto a floured surface and knead lightly. Roll out pastry and cut into rounds with a 9cm (3½ inch) fluted cutter.

Put equal amounts of mincemeat into half of the rounds and top with the remaining rounds, sealing well.

Place on a baking tray and brush with beaten egg. Bake in the centre of the oven at 220°C, 425°F, Gas No. 7 for 20 minutes.

Remove from the baking tray and dredge with caster sugar.

Date Tit Bits

225g 8oz **dates**
225g 8oz **rich tea biscuits**
225g 8oz **butter**
100g 4oz **caster sugar**
1 size 3 **egg, beaten**
5ml 1tsp **vanilla essence**
15ml 1tbsp **coconut, vermicelli**

Place the dates into the food processor and chop finely. Reserve.

Place the biscuits into the processor bowl and finely crumb.

In a saucepan melt the butter and sugar, add the chopped dates and boil together.

Remove from the heat, cool slightly, and add beaten egg and vanilla essence.

Return the date mixture to the processor bowl with the crushed biscuits and mix together well.

Press the mixture into a greased swiss roll tin and leave to cool.

Cut into squares and roll half in coconut and the rest in vermicelli.

Madeira Cake

175g 6oz **butter, softened**
175g 6oz **caster sugar**
3 size 3 eggs
225g 8oz **plain flour, sifted**
30ml 2tbsp **milk**
7.5ml 1½tsp **baking powder**
grated lemon rind of 1 medium lemon
10ml 2tsp **vanilla essence**

 Put all the ingredients into the processor bowl and mix together until very creamy.

Line a 20cm (8″) round cake tin with greaseproof paper and grease well.

Transfer the mixture into the prepared tin and smooth the top with a knife.

Bake in the centre of the oven at 170°C, 325°F, Gas No. 3 for 1½-1¾ hours, or until a wooden cocktail stick inserted into centre of cake comes out clean.

Leave in the tin for 5 minutes, then turn out onto a wire cooling rack.

Peel off greaseproof paper and allow cake to cool.

Ginger Biscuits

225g 8oz **plain flour**
5ml 1tsp **baking powder**
7.5ml 1½tsp **ground ginger**
5ml 1tsp **mixed spice**
100g 4oz **butter**
175g 6oz **caster sugar**
1 size 3 egg

 Place the flour, baking powder, ginger, mixed spice and butter in the processor bowl and process for 10 seconds.

Add the sugar and process for a further 5 seconds.

With the processor running add the egg down through the feed tube and mix to a soft dough.

Refrigerate overnight wrapped in cling film.

Roll out dough to 0·6cm (¼ inck) thickness, and cut into 5cm (2 inch) rounds (makes about 24).

Place on a greased baking tray well apart to allow for spreading and bake in the centre of the oven at 190°C, 375°F, Gas No. 5 for 10 minutes.

Cool on a wire cooling rack.

Vanilla Biscuits

225g 8oz **self raising flour**
pinch salt
125g 5oz **butter, cubed**
100g 4oz **caster sugar**
1 size 3 **egg, beaten**
10ml 2tsp **vanilla essence**
glacé cherries to decorate

 Place the flour, salt, butter and sugar into the processor bowl and process for 10 seconds.

With the machine still running add the beaten egg and vanilla essence and mix to a very stiff dough. (Add more egg if required).

Turn out onto a floured surface and knead the dough until smooth. Chill.

Roll out the dough fairly thinly and cut into rounds with a plain or flutted cutter.

Place on a greased baking tray and prick biscuits well with a fork. Place a halved glacé cherry into the centre of each biscuit. Chill.

Bake in the centre of the oven at 180°C, 350°F, Gas No. 4 for about 10 minutes or until a pale golden brown.

Allow to cool for 2-3 minutes before transferring onto a wire cooling rack.

Cornut Biscuits

Shortbread

50g 2oz **cornflakes**
2 size 3 egg whites
10ml 2tsp **vanilla essence**
150g 5oz **caster sugar**
75g 3oz **ground almonds**
16 blanched almonds for decoration

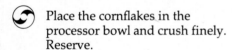 Place the cornflakes in the processor bowl and crush finely. Reserve.

Whisk the egg whites until very stiff.

Add the vanilla essence, sugar, ground almonds, and crushed cornflakes to the whisked egg whites.

Prepare a baking tray with greased greaseproof paper.

Take 5ml (1tsp) of the mixture and roll into a ball in the hands. Place on the baking tray and flatten slightly.

Place an almond on each biscuit and repeat with remaining mixture.

Bake in the centre of the oven at 190°C, 375°F, Gas No. 5 for 10 to 12 minutes until lightly brown.

When nearly cold remove from tin.

225g 8oz **butter**
100g 4oz **caster sugar**
275g 10oz **plain flour**
50g 2oz **semolina**
caster sugar for dusting

Place all the ingredients together in the food processor and mix together for 20 seconds. After 10 seconds stop the machine and scrape down ingredients.

Press mixture into a buttered 20cm 8" sandwich tin.

Prick well all over with a fork and pinch up edges.

Bake in the centre of the oven at 170°C, 325°F, Gas No. 3 for 40 minutes until a pale golden colour.

Leave in the tin for 5 minutes and then cut into triangles. Dredge with caster sugar and remove from tin when cold.

Preserves

Mixed Fruit Jam

375g 12oz **apples, peeled and cored**
750g 1½lb **pears, peeled and cored**
250g 8oz **grapes, deseeded**
150ml ¼pt **water**
1.4kg 3lb **granulated sugar**
25g 1oz **butter**

Place the fruit in the processor bowl and chop roughly.

Transfer the fruit to a saucepan with the water and bring to the boil.

Reduce the heat, cover pan, and simmer gently for 10 to 15 minutes

Add sugar and heat slowly, stirring all the time, until sugar dissolves.

Bring to the boil. Boil briskly for 10 to 15 minutes (or until setting point is reached).

Draw pan away from heat. Stir in butter to disperse scum.

Pot in warm sterilized jars. Cover with waxed paper and cellophane papers whilst hot.

Makes approximately 2·3kg (5lb) jam.

Autumn Marmalade

1.4kg 3lbs **Seville oranges**
2.5 litres 4½ pints **water**
juice of 2 large lemons
2.3kg 5lbs **sugar**

Scrub the fruit, cut in half and squeeze out the juice into a bowl. Tie the pips in a muslin bag.

Place the orange peel in batches into the food processor and chop coarsely.

Put the chopped peel into a heavy pan with the water, squeezed juice and muslin bag.

Bring to the boil and simmer until reduced by half. Squeeze muslin bag and remove.

Stir in the sugar and heat gently until dissolved.

Boil rapidly to setting point, and test by leaving a little marmalade on a cold saucer for a few minutes. If setting point is reached the marmalade will wrinkle if pushed with a finger.

Once the setting point is reached, allow marmalade to stand for 15 minutes.

Put in warm sterilized jars. Cover with waxed paper and cellophane paper whilst very hot.

Makes approximately 3.6kg (8lbs).

Fruit Chutney

900g 2lbs **cooking apples, peeled and cored**
700g 1½lb **onions, peeled and quartered**
100g 4oz **dried dates**
300g 11oz **raisins**
225g 8oz **soft brown sugar**
5ml 1tsp **ground ginger**
5ml 1tsp **salt**
400ml 14fl oz **malt vinegar**

 Finely chop the apples, onions and dates in 450g (1lb) batches in the processor bowl.

Place in a heavy pan and add the raisins, sugar, ginger, salt and vinegar.

Bring to the boil, then simmer until brown and thick (about 1 hour), stirring occasionally.

Bottle the chutney in sterilized jars.

Makes 1.8kg (4lbs).

Tomato Chutney

450g 1lb **onions, peeled and quartered**
2.3kg 5lb **ripe tomatoes, skinned**
275ml ½ pint **malt vinegar**
350g 12oz **granulated sugar**
15g ½oz **salt**
5ml 1tsp **cayenne pepper**
25g 1oz **mustard seeds**
15ml 1tbsp **whole allspice**

 Finely chop the onions, then tomatoes, in 450g (1lb) batches in processor bowl.

Place in a heavy pan with the vinegar, sugar, salt and cayenne pepper.

Tie the mustard seeds and allspice in a muslin bag and add to ingredients.

Bring all the ingredients to the boil, and simmer for 1 hour, stirring occasionally.

Remove the muslin bag and bottle the chutney in sterilised jars.

Makes 1.6kg (3½lbs).

RECIPE INDEX

A

Anchovy Pepper Dip 23
Apple Cake 84
Apple & Lemon Pudding 68
Apple Sauce 58
Apricot & Walnut Lamb 30
Autumn Marmalade 92

B

Bavarian Salad 47
Black Forest Gâteau 69
Blue Cheese Dressing 60
Boeuf en Croûte 29
Braised Cabbage 44
Bread 78
Bread Sauce 59

C

Cannelloni 35
Capon with Bacon & Celery Stuffing 31
Carribean Grill 55
Cheddarburgers 52
Cheese Sauce 60
Cheesy Chicken Balls 53
Cheesy Scalloped Potatoes 42
Cherry Cobblestone Cake 85
Chicken Liver Pâté 22
Chicken Loaf 54
Chicken Risotto 34
Chicken Soup 20
Chocolate & Banana Pudding 76
Christmas Pudding 73
Cordon Bleu Cake 71
Cornut Biscuits 90
Countrystyle Pork 33
Country Vegetable Omelette 51
Cream of Watercress Soup 18
Crusty Pork Chop 35
Curried Beef Pasties 52
Curried Rice Salad 46

D E

Date Titbits 87
Egg & Tuna Pickups 50

F

Fennel & Cheese Salad 46
Fish & Chips 38
Fish & Mushroom Bake 40
Fruit Chutney 93

G

Garlic Mushrooms 44
Gazpacho 19
Ginger Biscuits 88
Golden Fruit Pie 72

H

Harvest Hotpot 26
Hawaiian Baconburgers 50
Honey & Hazelnut Cheesecake 67

K L

Kofta Kebabs 27
Lamb Curry 32
Leeks in Mustard Sauce 43

M

Macaroni with Bacon Sauce 51
Madeira Cake 88
Mayonnaise 58
Malt Loaf 79
Midweek Salad 47
Mince Pies 86
Minestrone Soup 18
Mixed Cheese Spread 23
Mixed Fruit Jam 92
Mushroom & Courgette Flan 56
Mushroom Soup 19

O

Orange Coffee Gâteau 75

P

Parsley Sauce 59
Party Wheel Salad 48
Pashka 66
Peach & Chocolate Layer 62
Pineapple & Lemon Mousse 74
Plaice Curry 37
Plaice Roll-ups 39
Porkies in Onion Sauce 27
Portuguese Toasts 54

Q R

Quick Pan Pizza 53
Raspberry Soufflé 63
Ratatouille 45
Ribboned Trifle 74

S

Salami & Cheese Scones 81
Salami Dip 24
Savoury Cheese Crunch 55
Savoury Potato Patties 42
Savoury Stuffed Tomatoes 45
Scones 81
Shortbread 90
Smoked Mackerel Spread 22
Smokey Fish Crumble 36
Spicey Lamb Bake 26
Steak & Kidney Pie 28
Stilton & Celery Spread 24
Stir Fried Vegetables 43
Strawberry Cloud 65
Sweet Chicken Coleslaw 48
Swiss Roll 83

T

Tea Cakes 80
Tomato Chutney 93
Tomato Soup 20
Treacle Tart 70
Turkey Pâté 21

V W

Vanilla Biscuits 89
Veal & Bacon Loaf 34
Veal & Orange Terrine 21
Victoria Sponge 82
Walnut Ice Cream 64